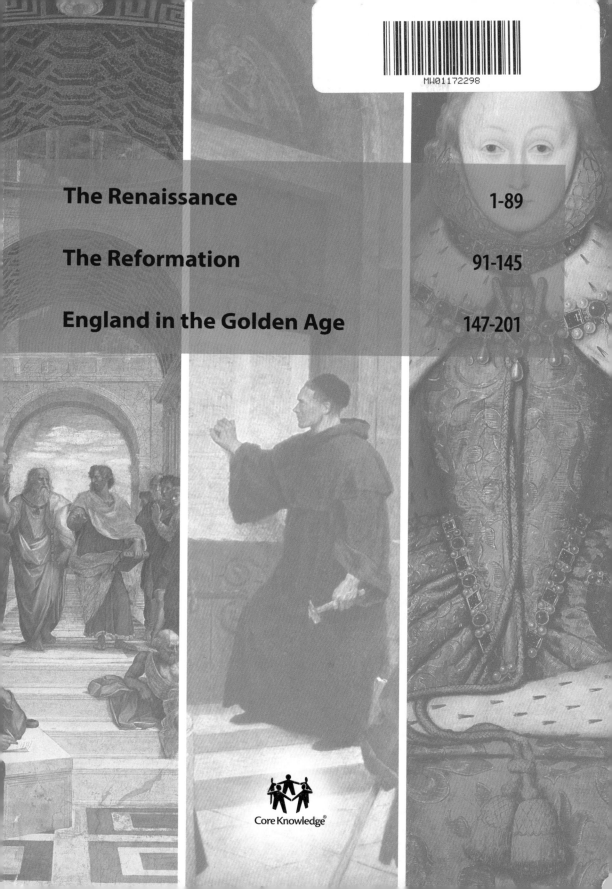

Core Knowledge®

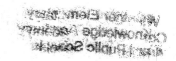

ISBN: 978-1-68380-274-7

The Renaissance

Table of Contents

Willa Cather Elementary
Core Knowledge Academy
Millard Public Schools

Reader
Core Knowledge History and Geography™

Chapter 1
A New Dawn

An Uncomfortable Visit In 1508, Desiderius Erasmus (/des*uh*dair*ee*us/ih*raz*mus/), the greatest European **scholar** of his age, journeyed from Holland to Venice, Italy. There, he stayed in the home of a leading printer, Aldus Manutius (/awl*dus/muh*noo*shee*us/).

The Big Question

What factors helped bring about the age known as the Renaissance?

Erasmus found his lodging most uncomfortable. The printer's house was drafty in winter and full of fleas and bed bugs in summer. As many as thirty scholars stayed in the printer's home at any one time. Manutius had little money to spend to make his guests comfortable. He provided the cook with moldy flour and served up meals of thin soup, hard cheese, and tough beef.

Why would Erasmus and other scholars travel long distances to endure uncomfortable conditions? These scholars all shared a desire to learn more about the civilizations of ancient Greece and Rome. They were fascinated with works of **classical literature**, including the philosophy of Plato (/plae*toe/), the poems of

Vocabulary

scholar, n. a person who specializes in a specific academic subject; an expert

"classical literature," (phrase), the works of ancient Greek and Roman writers

Erasmus saw that the rediscovery of ancient Greek and Roman written works opened up whole new worlds of thought.

Virgil, and the **orations** of Cicero (/sihs*uh*roe/). Throughout Italy, people were rediscovering and studying these works.

At the printer's dinner table, the scholars talked about Plato and Cicero, and exchanged ideas about ancient civilizations. They described their projects and dreams, and commented on one another's work. What's more, they did all of these things in the language of the ancient Greeks! Scholars who spoke any other language were fined.

The scholars were unhappy with the world in which they had grown up. They believed that they had been born in a less-cultured age in which people had forgotten about the great writers of Greece and Rome. These scholars rejected what they saw as the cold and lifeless teaching found in European universities of the day. They grumbled that the last several centuries had been remarkable mainly for their famines, plagues, warfare, ignorance, and superstition. Unfairly, some of them even labeled the previous one thousand years the "Dark Ages."

However, the dissatisfaction with the past made these men quite excited about what was happening in their own world. In Italy, people were rediscovering the wisdom of the ancient Greeks and Romans. Scholars, known as **humanists**, had been rummaging around in monasteries and cathedral libraries, digging up ancient Greek and Roman writings that had long been forgotten. Their name comes from the subjects we call the humanities, including history, languages, and literature.

Vocabulary

manuscript, n. a book or document written by hand

rhetoric, n. the skill of using words effectively in speaking or writing

These newly rediscovered **manuscripts** covered many topics. Some discussed philosophy or history. Others talked about literature, grammar, or **rhetoric**. Still others had to do with art and architecture. The humanists studied these manuscripts with loving care. They compared and corrected them, translated and explained them. At first, they painstakingly made copies of manuscripts by hand. After printing was invented, they gave precious manuscripts to a printer, like Erasmus's host, to publish.

For many humanists, there was a clear purpose behind the study of ancient manuscripts. By studying the beautiful writings of the ancient Greeks and ancient Romans, humanists hoped to become great writers, too. Great writers, poets, and speakers can shape the world in which they live. The humanists hoped to have influence over the views of the day.

These statues depict two of the great thinkers of ancient Greece: Plato and Socrates.

When Erasmus thought about the humanist movement, he thought he was taking part in the dawning of a brighter day. The other scholars around the dinner table were equally excited. They believed that they were participating in a rediscovery of the ancient civilizations of Greece and Rome, a rebirth of culture, literature, and the arts.

What All the Excitement Was About

What Erasmus and his fellow scholars were so excited about was the energetic period of change that we now call the Renaissance. This name comes from a French word that means rebirth. When we speak of the Renaissance, we refer to a period in history when a rediscovery of classical learning led to great achievements. These achievements affected not only literature, but also philosophy, education, architecture, sculpture, and painting.

The Renaissance began in Italy in the mid-1300s. For the next two centuries, the center of creative and scholarly activity moved from one major Italian city-state to another. Florence, Rome, and Valencia all played major roles in this movement. Later, in the 1500s and 1600s, the spirit of the Renaissance spread to other places in Europe, including Germany, France, Spain, and England.

Although the Renaissance began with the rediscovery of old manuscripts, it didn't end there. The humanists studied works of ancient art, architecture, and literature. These studies led to increased interest in all these fields. Soon, people were examining ancient Greek and Roman statues and marveling at their beauty.

Renaissance sculptors tried to capture the same qualities in their own creations. As the years went by, more and more of them modeled their works on ancient Greek and Roman examples instead of on the more recent work of medieval artists. Architects studied ancient buildings and used them as models for new structures. Renaissance poets tried to write poems as skillfully as the ancient poets had. Painters sought out new subjects to paint, inspired by people and ideas of the ancient world. All these artists were using old art to create new art.

This sculpture is based on a Greek statue of Atlas, who bore the world on his shoulders.

Important Renaissance Figures

Over time, the Renaissance spread across Europe. In the early 1600s, the greatest writer of the English Renaissance, William Shakespeare, looked to the ancient world for inspiration for some of his plays. He wrote about Julius Caesar and Antony and Cleopatra.

Cowards die many times before their deaths;
The valiant never taste of death but once.
Of all the wonders that I yet have heard,
It seems to me most strange that men should fear;
Seeing that death, a necessary end,
Will come when it will come.

Julius Caesar, Act 2, Scene 2

Shakespeare and Erasmus are just two of many Renaissance figures who are still widely admired today. Others include the Italian artists Raphael (/rah*fah*el/), Leonardo da Vinci (/duh*vihn*chee/), and Michelangelo (/mie*kul*an*juh*loe/); the Italian political writer Machiavelli (/mahk*e*uh*vel*ee/); and the great Spanish novelist Cervantes (/sur*van*teez/). Indeed, perhaps no age in history has produced more celebrated artists and thinkers than the Renaissance. In this unit you will learn about the greatest of these figures. But before we turn to individuals, let's look at some reasons the Renaissance began where it did.

Italy the Innovator

As you read the opening paragraphs of this chapter, you may have wondered why the Renaissance began in Italy and not in a place such as England or Germany. Scholars have argued about that question for years and have suggested some reasons Italy led the way.

For one thing, Italy had been the center of the ancient Roman Empire. The ruins of that great empire surrounded the people of Italy: crumbling walls and toppled columns, arenas and temples overrun with weeds, once-splendid roads long ago fallen into disrepair. These reminders ensured that ancient Rome was never entirely forgotten.

Commerce also helped pave the way for the Italian Renaissance. Italy is a boot-shaped peninsula, jutting into the Mediterranean Sea. Trading ships sailed back and forth

> **Vocabulary**
>
> **commerce**, n. the buying and selling of goods and services

You can see how the ruins of the Forum, a public meeting place in ancient Rome, influenced late Renaissance buildings such as the church in the background in this photograph.

across the Mediterranean. They traveled from Western Europe to the Middle East and from northern Africa to southern Europe. With its central location, Italy was in a good position to profit from this trade.

During the Renaissance there was no central government in Italy. Instead, the peninsula was divided into more than 250 city-states. A city-state was like a small country. At its heart was a city that was the center of government and business. It also included the countryside with its farms and villages. Most of the city-states were tiny, but some, for example, Florence, Venice, Milan, and Genoa were larger. Many were located on the sea, or on rivers near the sea. They used their advantageous locations to gain wealth by trading with other lands. Competition among the city-states led to further improvements as each city-state worked hard to attract the best traders.

As trade grew, a new merchant class sprang up in prosperous city-states. Many merchants grew wealthy. Some of them used their wealth to support humanistic scholarship and the arts. In addition to these wealthy merchants, many nobles and church leaders acted as supporters of the arts. Without them, there probably would not have been a Renaissance.

Members of the new merchant class were eager to give their male children an education that would prepare them for success in business and in running their city-states. Merchants wanted their sons to know how to keep good business records. They also wanted them to know

the law and to be skilled at negotiation and **diplomacy** so that they could deal effectively with trading partners. Because these young men would be traveling, they needed to learn history and geography. These merchants also wanted their sons to learn about religion and good morals. Some merchants even wanted their sons to learn ancient Greek and Latin so that they could read the best ancient books. These ambitions led to higher educational standards. Often, merchants hired humanists to teach their children, and this helped spread a love of the humanities throughout the city-states. In contrast, in northern Europe, education was generally in the hands of the Church.

Increasingly, Italians came into contact with people from distant lands and of differing faiths. Diversity also increased at home. While most Renaissance Italians were Christians, many city-states also included Jewish families. Business trips often sent Italian merchants to regions of northern Europe. Trade also brought them into contact with Muslims from the east and the south. Contact with Muslims was especially rewarding because, during the Middle Ages, Islamic scholars had preserved many ancient Greek manuscripts.

In addition to preserving valuable ancient manuscripts, Islamic scholars wrote new works on medicine, astronomy, philosophy, and mathematics. Their works became widely used in European universities and contributed greatly to the expansion of knowledge.

There is another way in which Islam contributed to the Renaissance. In the 1300s and 1400s, Ottoman Turks completed their takeover of the Byzantine Empire. Some Byzantine scholars fled to Italy. They brought with them valuable Greek manuscripts. They also brought a thorough knowledge of the ancient Greek language in which the texts were written, and they brought their own new ideas.

An Important Invention

Once the Renaissance began, it was greatly advanced by an important German invention: the printing press. Around the year 1450, Johannes Gutenberg (/yoe*hahn*es/goot*en*burg) developed a new way of printing books and papers. Gutenberg **devised** a system of

> **Vocabulary**
>
> **devise,** v. to come up with an idea, plan, or invention

movable letter stamps. These stamps could be quickly arranged to form words and sentences. They were then inked and pressed onto paper. Before this invention, writings had to be copied by hand. This was a slow and expensive process. Humanists had been willing to copy manuscripts because they were so excited about their discoveries. But even the most energetic scholar could make only a handful of copies of any given manuscript. Gutenberg's invention made it possible to make many copies of books, newspapers, and pamphlets quickly and at low cost. The knowledge that the humanists had gathered could be easily spread and shared.

Use of movable type and the printing press spread quickly in Italy. By 1500, Italy boasted more printing presses than any other

During the Renaissance, knowledge spread because of print shops such as this one, which could produce many volumes in a short time.

country in Europe. Printers such as Aldus Manutius, whom Erasmus visited, helped spread the important texts of ancient Greece and Rome far and wide.

Many factors helped bring about the Italian Renaissance. Among them were the ruins of ancient Rome and the inspiration they provided. The prosperity of city-states and the rise of merchants and other wealthy people also contributed. Increased interest in education and greater understanding of foreign cultures also played a part in the Italian Renaissance. Other factors include the presence of Byzantine scholars with Greek manuscripts and the printing press. This is only a short list of the many causes that helped shape a very important time in history.

Chapter 2
From Artisan to Artist

The Artist Elevated When we visit an art museum, we are not surprised that an artist has put his or her name on the canvas or chiseled it into the stone. Nor are we surprised that a museum might advertise an exhibit of work from a particular artist.

The Big Question

What were some of the changes that occurred during the Renaissance for artists and the work they produced?

We do not find it unusual that the architect's name is cut into the cornerstone of a building. When we hear a piece of music, we usually also expect to learn who composed it.

But it was not always this way. Before the Renaissance, painters did not generally sign their works. Architects did not typically carve their names on the buildings they built. Musicians were rarely given credit for music they composed.

In the medieval period, artists did not have the status that they enjoy today. They were thought of artisans or craftspeople. The way people saw it, painters and sculptors worked with their hands, just like a shoemaker, baker, or bricklayer. They often worked for low wages

As with many works of medieval art, the name of the person who created this religious painting is unknown.

just as other craftspeople did. A medieval artist created precisely the work his employer paid him to produce. He didn't even think of signing it.

Medieval artists were like printers; they were paid to do a job.

The relatively low status of sculptors and painters was reflected by the guilds, or trade associations, to which they belonged. In Florence for example, sculptors were members of the Guild of Masons. That's because, like **masons**, sculptors worked with stone. Painters got many of their paints and supplies from **apothecaries** (/uh*path*uh*ker*eez/). So, in Florence, they were members of the Guild of Doctors and Apothecaries.

A Change of Status

During the Renaissance, the status of artists changed dramatically. The humanists discovered that the ancient Greeks and Romans had respect for artists and architects. When beautiful Greek and Roman statues were put on display, people of the Renaissance began to see why.

16

People began to realize that if artists could create such beautiful objects, they must have a rare skill.

The humanists also unearthed manuscripts that described forgotten artistic techniques. They imitated ancient works and then created impressive works of their own. Renaissance artists mastered new techniques and principles to give **form** and structure to their work.

Gradually, a change took place. Painters and sculptors began to think of themselves as artists rather than artisans. They were creators rather than craftspeople. They began taking credit for their creations by signing them. The best artists also began to charge handsome fees, particularly in the late 1400s and early 1500s. A few great artists even felt free to change or ignore the directions of the people who hired them to create their works. This was a sign of the rising confidence and status of the artists.

Some painters and sculptors even began inserting likenesses of themselves in their works. Lorenzo Ghiberti (/loh*ren*tsoe/ ghee*ber*tee/) was a successful bronze sculptor in Florence in the first half of the 1400s. He included a self-portrait in one of the magnificent doors he created for the **baptistery** of the cathedral in Florence. Sandro Botticelli (/san*dro/baht*uh*chel*ee), a fifteenth-century painter from Florence, placed his own likeness in one of his paintings of the *Adoration of the Magi*.

Botticelli's *Adoration of the Magi* shows wise men visiting the baby Jesus (center), but it also includes a self-portrait of the artist (lower right).

In the painting Botticelli stands to one side, looking straight out at the viewer.

Artists were not alone in exhibiting themselves through artwork. Much more frequently, important people **commissioned** portraits and sculptures of themselves. Leading families hired artists to create family portraits. They did this to promote their families and highlight their importance.

Portrait Painting

Artists placed increasing emphasis on **realism** in art during this time. Medieval painters had paid little attention to realistic detail. Figures in their pictures were recognizable as human beings, but they

generally didn't look like anyone in particular. Now Renaissance artists began to strive for more realism. They wanted to capture the exact appearance of a person in a particular situation. They wanted their figures to have facial expressions that revealed true emotions.

The Natural World

Renaissance painters also began to pay more attention to the natural world. Most medieval art was made for churches and other religious settings. Painters liked to fill the spaces around the figures in a painting with gold leaf. This was to show their love and respect for the figures and stories in these paintings. They wanted just enough detail so that anyone who saw the work of art would know easily what it was about. During the Renaissance, people began wanting paintings that looked lively and more like the world around them. They also wanted works that showed off the skill of the artist.

The architect Brunelleschi (/broo*nel*les*kee/) worked in Florence and Rome in the early 1400s. He, along with a fellow humanist and architect named Alberti (/al*behr*tee/), made important advances in the creation of realistic art. They discovered a mathematical formula that, when applied to a painting or drawing, seemed to give the image depth. When an artist used this formula in his work, the end result would look more realistic. Both men were inspired by an essay on architecture written by an ancient Roman writer named Vitruvius (/vih*troo*vee*us/). Vitruvius described how buildings and other objects painted on a flat surface could appear to "advance and recede"—come forward and extend backward. This effect made a painting look more realistic and **three-dimensional**. Though inspired by the ancients, Brunelleschi and Alberti invented the technique of **perspective**.

> ### Vocabulary
>
> **three-dimensional,** adj. describing an object that has depth as well as width and height, especially a painting that appears not to be flat
>
> **perspective,** n. a technique used to make something that is flat appear to have depth, in addition to height and width

Brunelleschi taught the principles of perspective, and Alberti wrote a book about their findings. In many ways this book was the first of its kind on the subject of painting. Many other Renaissance painters mastered this technique.

Renaissance painters were now able to place realistic figures in realistic backgrounds. Indeed, they began to create spaces that made viewers feel as if they could step through the painting and into the world it showed.

Brunelleschi and Alberti's discovery of perspective was a good example of how Renaissance artists managed to go forward by looking backward in time. The two men learned what they could from the ancient writers and in so doing were able to move forward. Their findings helped bring about a great flowering of the arts in Florence.

Raphael's painting, *School of Athens*, uses perspective to make the viewer feel as if he or she is looking down a long corridor—even though the picture itself is flat.

Chapter 3
The Cradle of the Renaissance

The City on the Arno To experience all the wonders of the Renaissance, one had only to visit the city of Florence in the 1400s. Its economy, artists, architects, writers, and philosophers all helped make Florence a model of Renaissance culture.

The Big Question

How did the success of merchants and bankers during the Renaissance benefit artists?

Florence was well-positioned to become a center of trade and commerce. Like the other important Italian cities of that age, Florence enjoyed important geographic advantages. It was founded in Roman times on flat land alongside the Arno River. To the west, the river gave it access to the sea. The city was accessible in other directions through mountain passes.

By the time of the Renaissance, Florence had grown large and rich. Compared to other Italian city-states, it was politically **stable**.

Vocabulary

stable, adj. unlikely to go through changes

Florence—shown here in an image from the late 1400s—was at the heart of the Renaissance.

Like other cities, Florence did suffer from problems such as violence, overcrowding, and disease. In contrast to many other cities, however, its commercial success and its form of government allowed Florence to slowly overcome these challenges. The knowledge gained in solving these problems benefited other European countries, too.

Near the height of its influence, in 1472, Florence boasted a powerful **merchant class** that was the envy of rival city-states. And although Florence is best remembered for its painters, sculptors, architects, and scholars, these artistic successes depended on the city's commercial success. After all, it was wealthy Florentine merchants who served as **patrons** and made the arts possible.

Florence became an intellectual center as well. The leading families in Florence turned to the study of ancient Roman authors. These classical writers told of the Roman **heritage** of great political, commercial, and military successes. Such stories appealed to the rising merchant class. A deep appreciation of all aspects of classical civilization developed in Florence. This helped create an atmosphere in which bold political and artistic ideas could flourish.

> ## Vocabulary
>
> **"merchant class,"** (phrase), a social class made up of wealthy and powerful merchants
>
> **patron,** n. a person who gives money or other support to someone, such as an artist
>
> **heritage,** n. something that is inherited by one person or group from an older person or group

Wool and Banking

Florence's wealth during the Renaissance depended in large part on two industries: wool and banking. It is estimated that at the wool industry's peak, about one of three Florentines worked in the wool business. The names of the city's streets tell of wool's importance. There were, for example, the Street of Shearers, the Street of Cauldrons (giant pots in which wool was cleaned and treated), and the Road of Dyers. Each

This image shows the production of wool, which was the foundation of a thriving trade that helped make Florence a wealthy city.

street was dedicated to a process used to turn raw wool into the cloth that Florentine merchants sold throughout the world.

The leading Florentine merchants involved in the wool business were members of the Wool Guild and the Calimala Guild. Members of the Calimala Guild controlled the importing, dyeing, and finishing of cloth. This trade association was the most important and powerful guild in Florence. Many cloth merchants were also members of the Guild of Bankers and Moneychangers. Quite often, it was these people and their influential families who ran the government of Florence.

The structure of the government of Florence was complex. Inspired by the examples of Greece and Rome, Florence considered itself a republic. In Florence's republic, power was in the hands of a ruling class of citizens rather than a single monarch. Incredibly, leading families in Florence chose government officials by picking names out of a bag. Of course, those eligible to have their names placed in the bag were the most influential people in Florence. Citizens were governed by a council made up of rich and educated men who represented them.

A Powerful Family

Banking made a few merchants as rich and powerful as the nobility for the first time in history. Imitating the nobility, these bankers and merchants became patrons of the arts.

No Florentine family was more rich and powerful than the Medici (/med*ee*chee/) family. The Medici were wool merchants who rose to power largely because of their banking business. By 1417, the family had bank branches in several important cities in Italy as well as in key European cities. Perhaps most important, the Medici were the moneylenders to the pope, the leader of Christians in Europe.

In the 1400s, Cosimo de' Medici was the powerful head of Florence's most powerful family.

26

They enjoyed a profitable relationship with the papal office responsible for collecting and spending church **revenues**.

In 1429, Cosimo (/koe*see*moe/) de' Medici became leader of the Medici family after the death of his father. Like his father, Cosimo possessed a genius for banking. In time, the government of Florence came to depend on the Medici banking operation for the generous loans it made.

Cosimo de' Medici soon became the leading citizen of the republic. He rarely held government office himself, but he was able to ensure that his friends often held office. Through them, he maintained control of the government.

The education Medici received as a young man had created a deep respect for ancient Greece and Rome. From his youth, Cosimo paid agents to search for classical manuscripts abroad. He employed a staff of about forty-five men to copy for his library any manuscripts he was unable to purchase.

Later in life, Medici spent large sums on classical art and architecture. He funded many architects, sculptors, and painters, including the artist Brunelleschi. In addition to contributing to the discovery of the technique of perspective, Brunelleschi was a brilliant architect. One of his most lasting works can be seen in the Santa Maria del Fiore (/san*tuh/*mah*ree*uh/del/fyoh*ree/) cathedral in Florence, often called the Duomo (/dwoh*moh/).

Building of the cathedral began in 1294. Many great artists and sculptors worked on the building before it was completed in 1436.

You can appreciate why it took more than 100 years to build the great cathedral in Florence.

In 1415, Brunelleschi was asked to design and build the dome for the cathedral. Daringly, Brunelleschi's design included no interior supports to hold up the tons of stone and bricks from which the dome was built. Brunelleschi's brilliant planning and calculation ensured that the dome would be able to support itself.

Brunelleschi became known as the first genius of the Renaissance. His dome was considered the greatest engineering feat of the time. Once again, a new masterpiece had been inspired by the ancient world, in this instance the Pantheon in Rome.

Upon Cosimo de' Medici's death in 1464, his son Piero (/pee*ehr*oe/) assumed leadership of the famous family. Piero lived only five years more. He was succeeded by his son Lorenzo the Magnificent.

Lorenzo the Magnificent

Lorenzo (/lohr*enz*oe/) de' Medici strove to make Florence a center of festivals and pageants. He commissioned artists to create works for himself and for the public events he organized. But his greatest impact was in encouraging other leaders to hire the city's artists.

During nine years of relative peace and prosperity, Lorenzo de' Medici was able to build and use political power, as his grandfather had. In 1478 he was the victim of a plot hatched by a rival family in Florence. The plan was apparently backed by Pope Sixtus IV. Lorenzo, who some believed was becoming too powerful, survived an assassination attempt and then a war with the pope's forces. He returned to Florence in 1480. To stay safe, he surrounded himself with armed guards.

For the next twelve years, Lorenzo worked to make Florence Italy's capital of art and learning. He brought the most famous teachers of Italy to the city-state. He spent large sums on art and books.

He founded a school to train boys in art but also in the humanities. The sculptor, architect, and painter Michelangelo spent four years in Lorenzo's school. Michelangelo became a member of the Medici household and showed his patron the results of his work each day.

Unfortunately, Lorenzo did not have the same interest in the Medici banking business. He also did not have the same business skills as his grandfather. As a result, the bank's fortunes declined. This led to a decline of the fortunes of Florence itself. Trade with the East decreased. The city's cloth merchants found themselves unable to compete with cloth merchants in Flanders, in present-day Belgium. Florence's role as a center of art and learning did not end, but other cities were now better able to compete with it.

Giovanni Mannozzi's painting shows Lorenzo de' Medici, a great patron of art, surrounded by artists as he admires a Michelangelo sculpture.

Lorenzo died in 1492. He was succeeded by his son Piero, who was forced into **exile** by a foreign invader just two years later. The Medici family was able to regain power in Florence in 1512. But now the family's influence expanded into a different area. The head of the Medici family at this time arranged for his son Giovanni (/joe*vahn*ee/) to be named a **cardinal** in the Catholic Church. Giovanni would eventually become Pope Leo X. It would be in Rome that Leo X would continue the Medici tradition of promoting Renaissance art and learning.

Chapter 4
Rome and the Renaissance Popes

The Splendor of the Popes The popes who led the Roman Catholic Church occupied a unique and powerful place in Renaissance Italy—indeed, in the world. They considered themselves the successors of St. Peter, one of the twelve apostles of Jesus and the first leader of the Christian Church.

The Big Question

How did the Roman Catholic Church use the many talents of Renaissance artists?

The popes were responsible for leading and protecting Christian believers. In fact, the popes managed the largest organization in Europe: the Roman Catholic Church.

A pope's authority reached far beyond religion. In addition to leading the Church administration, he was also the ruler of central Italy, an area called the Papal States. As rulers of this territory, the popes enjoyed political independence.

St. Peter's Basilica became a symbol of the power of Rome.

The territories under **papal** control had grown over the course of many centuries. By the time of the Renaissance, the pope ruled the largest area in Italy except for

the Kingdom of Naples. The pope governed these territories from Rome, and in the mid-1400s, the Vatican became the papal residence.

Pope Nicholas V is usually credited with bringing the ideas of the Renaissance to Rome. Nicholas was a dedicated humanist. He welcomed teachers, historians, and thinkers to Rome. He rebuilt and repaired many of the city's buildings and bridges, and hired the greatest artists for the work. Pope Nicholas wanted the artists to use their talents to show the power and splendor of the Roman Catholic Church. In this way, he made Rome more attractive to tourists and pilgrims. He also helped make the Church and Roman merchants rich.

Many of Pope Nicholas's successors were also humanists. Pope Sixtus IV improved Rome's roads and buildings. He added more than a thousand books to the Vatican library, built the Sistine Chapel in the Vatican, and brought the best artists to Rome to add to its beauty.

Pope Julius II, like his uncle Sixtus IV, was also interested in rebuilding Rome. He was a good administrator and military leader. These skills helped him gain back authority over the Papal States, which had been weakened for a while.

Also like his uncle, Julius II expanded the Vatican library. To celebrate the Church's glory and its teachings, he invited important artists to come to Rome. The artists applied their skills to existing Church buildings.

Vocabulary

fresco, n. a type of painting made on wet plaster

They also created beautiful new ones. He hired the young painter Raphael to paint **frescoes** on the walls of the papal apartments. Julius II also hired Michelangelo, first to design his tomb and then to paint the ceiling of the Sistine Chapel.

This fresco is by the Renaissance great Raphael, one of the most celebrated painters of the era.

St. Peter's Basilica

In the fourth century, Emperor Constantine began building a church in Rome on the site where it was believed St. Peter had been buried. That church stood for twelve hundred years. In 1506, under Pope Julius II,

Vocabulary

basilica, n. a type of large Christian church, often built in the shape of a cross

work began on a larger, magnificent new **basilica** to replace the crumbling original structure. This larger new building would allow for a greater number of people, especially pilgrims.

St. Peter's Basilica was not completed for 120 years. Great artists, such as Michelangelo and Raphael, applied their skills to this massive project. Church leaders and artists worked together to

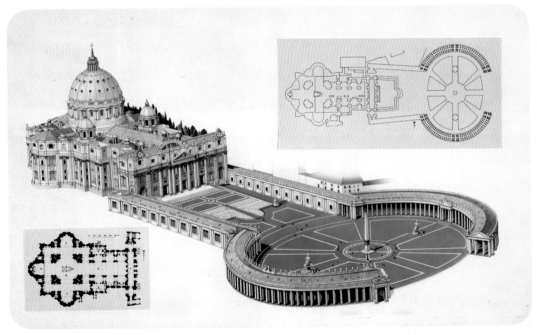

The Square in front of St. Peter's was built to hold the huge crowds that came, and still come, for important papal ceremonies.

create one of the most remarkable and beautiful buildings in the world. This project showed the power and status of the Church.

Pope Julius II was succeeded by Lorenzo de' Medici's son Giovanni, who took the name Leo X. His election in 1513 came the year after the Medici family was restored to power in Florence. As pope, Leo X showed both a love of art and a love of luxury. Like his father, Leo sponsored festivals and pageants, starting with his own magnificent coronation. He hired the best artists, including both Michelangelo and Raphael, and welcomed scholars and poets to the Vatican.

Leo's efforts were expensive, especially the construction of St. Peter's Basilica. To pay the high costs, Leo X raised taxes and borrowed huge sums of money. Like popes before him, he allowed people to pay money in return for positions of authority in the Church. And, in 1514, he extended throughout much of Europe a money-raising effort that had begun in Italy: He allowed the granting of religious pardons, called **indulgences,** for money donations. The Church taught that sins, or mistakes, would prevent people from going to heaven if not forgiven by the Church. If a person committed a sin, the Church asked him or her to do something to make up for the mistake—a penance. The Church also taught that indulgences could release people from part of their penance. But—and this was important—the indulgence would not work unless the person also confessed

> **Vocabulary**
>
> **indulgence,** n. the removal or reduction of certain punishments for sin, linked to a special act of penance

the sin to a priest, truly felt sorry, and received forgiveness. So, the indulgence removed part of the penance. But the "sinner" still had to perhaps pray, do good works, and even donate money for a specific cause. When Pope Leo X extended the practice of indulgences across Europe, he increased the Church's ability to raise money in this way. Some people strongly objected to this practice. These objections, along with other issues, would help trigger what was later called the Protestant Reformation. This event resulted in divisions in the Christian Church.

Last of the Renaissance Popes

Clement VII was the nephew of Lorenzo de' Medici and cousin of Pope Leo X. He became pope in 1523. Clement shared his family's love of the arts. But he made unwise alliances in his effort to protect the independence of the Papal States. His poor decisions left the Vatican vulnerable. Enemies were able to attack Rome in 1527. They looted churches and monasteries, and destroyed many manuscripts in the Vatican library. They damaged some of the artwork the popes had commissioned.

Clement made peace with his enemies and was returned to power in 1528. Rome was rebuilt and continued to be a center for art and architecture.

Leo X, a member of the Medici family, hired many Renaissance artists to capture the splendor of the Catholic Church.

Chapter 5
Venice: Jewel of the Adriatic

A Glittering City Venice, a city built on 117 small islands on the coast of northern Italy, was the Western world's leading commercial center in 1500.

The Big Question

Why was Venice known as the "Jewel of the Adriatic" during the Renaissance period?

Venice became the great trading and maritime power of the Renaissance.

Venice's islands, located in a **lagoon** connected to the Adriatic Sea, were divided by more than one hundred fifty canals. The islands were connected by more than four hundred bridges. Many of its buildings rested on pillars driven into the mud. Because of its location, Venice was safe from an attack. Enemy ships found it impossible to move in the shallow waters. Venice also had a strong navy, which was the basis of its sizable wealth.

The people of Venice, called Venetians (/vuh*nee*shunz/), were proud of their splendid city. Visitors marveled at the architecture. They were also amazed by the rich **furnishings** found in the homes of the wealthy people of the city.

How did Venice become so prosperous? Like Florence, Venice built its wealth mostly on trade. Over two centuries, Venetians managed an extensive trading empire. They were determined to carry on their trading activities and acquisition of wealth without interference.

Venetian merchants visited ports in Syria and Egypt and along the coast of the Black Sea. There, Venetian merchants traded for herbs, spices, and dyes from the Far East, and for cottons, silks, and silver goods from the Middle East. In exchange, Venetian merchants offered the many products of their own industries, such as glass, **textiles,** and jewelry.

Protecting this trade was vital to the Venetians. During the 1200s and 1300s, Venice established ports and island strongholds along the Adriatic Sea, leading to the Mediterranean Sea. They defended

Vocabulary
....
galley, n. a flat-bottomed boat with both sails and oars

these strongholds with a formidable navy. The navy's flat-bottomed **galleys** were built in Venice. Shipbuilding employed about two thousand Venetians. It was probably the largest industry of its time.

Venice also wanted free access to trading partners to the north of the Alps, the mountain range that stood between their city and much of Europe. So, during the 1400s, Venice conquered

Venetian merchants meet to discuss the price of their goods.

territories to its north and west. These territories included Padua (/paj*oo*uh/) and Verona (/vuh*roe*nuh/) in present-day Italy. These conquests assured safe overland passage for Venetian merchants seeking trade in Germany and elsewhere in northern Europe.

Late in the 1400s and early in the 1500s, Venice suffered some military setbacks. First, Turkish forces seized many of Venice's eastern territories. The Turks forced Venice to pay a yearly fee for trading in Turkish ports. Then, an alliance of Italian, German, French, and Spanish forces, headed by Pope Julius I, recaptured some of the Italian territories Venice had conquered. Over time, Venice won back some of these territories, though at great financial and human cost. Its efficient navy gave it the military force needed to defend its trading empire, at least for a while longer.

This painting from the 1500s suggests the size of the Venetian naval fleet.

Republican Government

Venice, like Florence, was not a monarchy but a republic. The government was controlled by the city-state's leading families. The head of the government was called the doge (/doej/). The title comes from a Latin word meaning leader. Members of the Greater Council chose a doge to serve for life. From its members, the Greater Council also selected people to serve in other government bodies. These included a **senate** and a committee for public safety. Although the doge was Venice's **chief of state**, the power to rule in the end lay in the hands of the **council** and the other governmental bodies whose members it selected.

As in most other republics of the time, not all Venetians could participate in government. At the end of the 1200s, the Greater Council passed a new law. It said that only male descendants of men who had sat on the council before 1297 were allowed to be members. The name of everyone eligible was written down in what became known as the *Book of Gold*. Only about two hundred families were named in the book. They became **hereditary** rulers of Venice.

In the late 1400s and early 1500s, the wealth of merchant traders allowed Venice to compete with Florence and Rome for leadership of the Renaissance. Aside from its wealth, Venice benefited from the arrival of foreign scholars. In 1453, Ottoman Turks conquered Constantinople, capital of the Byzantine Empire. Many scholars living there fled and made their way into Europe. Many moved to Venice. They brought both their knowledge and precious manuscripts from ancient Greece.

Printing Advances

One of Venice's most notable contributions to classical learning was its encouragement of the printing craft. By 1500 the city-state alone had more than two hundred printing presses. Because many printers were scholars, they devoted themselves to finding and publishing classical manuscripts, particularly those from ancient Greece.

The printer whom Erasmus visited in Venice, Aldus Manutius, was dedicated to his craft. Although he died exhausted and poor, Manutius succeeded in enriching his own age and ages to come. He did this by using the printing press as a way to preserve ancient heritage.

Venice's Greatest Artist

Venice was known for many different types of art during the Renaissance. Its greatest fame, however, was for its painting. No Venetian painter was more respected than Tiziano Vecelli (/tee*syah*noe/vay*chel*lee/), known familiarly as Titian (/tihsh*un/).

Venice boasted many printing presses, which helped spread Renaissance knowledge and learning.

Born around 1488, he was brought to Venice at age nine or ten to study with some of the city's most important painters. When his long career came to an end in 1576, he had surpassed them all.

Titian was noted for his appeal to the emotions and senses. His use of color and oil paints gave his works a rich and luxurious feel.

Also famous is Titian's series of portraits of the Holy Roman Emperor Charles V, who became his patron. Titian

Titian painted this portrait of Isabella d'Este, a prominent woman of the Renaissance.

also painted portraits of Francis I of France and Philip II of Spain. Emperor Charles V admired Titian so much that it is reported he once picked up the artist's paintbrush when Titian dropped it on the floor. This was something unheard of for an emperor to do for a mere commoner!

Decline of Venice

Over time, Venice lost ground as the world's leading trading power. The Turks successfully challenged Venetian dominance in the Mediterranean. Portuguese explorers found new sea routes to the Far East, shifting trade away from the Mediterranean and the Middle East to the Atlantic Ocean and beyond. Venice remained an independent state until the end of the 1700s. But its position in relation to world trade and commerce would never again be as strong as it was in the glory days of the Renaissance.

Chapter 6
Leonardo da Vinci

Imagining Things That Are to Be

A young man named Leonardo da Vinci applied for a job with the ruling Duke of Milan (/mih*lan/). To convince the duke of his worth, Leonardo sent a lengthy description of the services he could offer. Today, we would call that description his **résumé** (/reh*zoo*mae/).

The Big Question

Why might Leonardo da Vinci be described as a symbol of the Renaissance?

Vocabulary

résumé, n. a listing of a person's skills, training, and achievements

"jack-of-all-trades," (idiom), a person who can do a large number of jobs or tasks

visionary, n. a person who is able to imagine and plan for the future

In the description of his skills, Leonardo explained his ideas for the creation of new bridges, weapons, and other devices. If we knew nothing else about Leonardo but his description of his skills, we might conclude he was an engineer or soldier. In fact, he was also one of the foremost artists of the age—or any age.

Like many great Renaissance artists, Leonardo was a **jack-of-all-trades**. He was a sculptor, a painter, a designer, and a scientist. Most of all, he was a **visionary**.

Throughout his life, Leonardo made sketches of machines and devices, many of which were later developed and used.

Vocabulary

apprentice, n. a person who trains for a job or skill by working under the supervision and guidance of an expert in the field

Leonardo was born in 1452 near the village of Vinci, about sixty miles from Florence. When he was about fifteen, his father took him to a famous artist in Florence. He persuaded the artist to make his son an **apprentice**.

Apprentices observed the master at work and did whatever simple tasks the master gave them. Gradually, apprentices began to learn the skills of painting, designing, and sculpting from their master.

The work of apprentices was demanding. They rarely had days off. They spent long hours copying drawings so they could become familiar with the master's style. In fact, although a painting might bear the master's name, it was in many cases an apprentice who actually completed the work.

Leonardo spent less time as an apprentice than most boys. And, as time would reveal, he was spectacularly talented. According to one legend, Leonardo's master asked him to paint an angel in a painting for one of the master's patrons. The master found Leonardo's

Leonardo da Vinci created this self-portrait.

work so beautiful that he knew he could never equal it. He then gave up painting to concentrate on sculpture. The story may not be totally true, but its underlying message is a fact: Leonardo was an artist of rare ability.

About five years after he began his apprenticeship, Leonardo opened his own workshop in Florence. Leonardo did some remarkable work during this time. But he also began a habit of starting works that he would not complete.

The Master of All Trades

Leonardo was about thirty years old when he sent his résumé to the duke of Milan. He had heard that the duke was looking for a military engineer, a painter, an architect, and a sculptor. Leonardo offered to fill all the positions himself. The duke would not be disappointed. During his seventeen-year stay in Milan, Leonardo completed some of his greatest work.

After he arrived in Milan, the duke asked him to paint a picture of the Last Supper on the wall of a monastery dining room. This represented the final meal Jesus shared with his twelve apostles. The artist labored for three years on the project. It was said that the **prior** complained that the artist was taking too much time to complete the work.

> **Vocabulary**
>
> **prior,** n. a priest who helps lead a monastery

When the duke asked Leonardo why it was taking so long, the artist explained that he was having trouble painting the faces of Jesus and of the apostle Judas, who would betray Jesus. He could not imagine how to paint a face so beautiful that it was worthy of Jesus, nor could he imagine how to paint the features of a man as horrible as Judas. The story goes that Leonardo cunningly suggested that he might use the face of the prior as a model for Judas. Word may have gotten back to the prior because, from that time on, Leonardo was able to work at his painting without any complaints from the prior.

When Leonardo completed *The Last Supper*, it was recognized as a **masterpiece**. The painting remains in its original place today. But it has suffered greatly over the years from such things as dampness, neglect, and natural

deterioration. Nonetheless, many people believe it is the greatest painting that the Renaissance had produced up to that point.

Leonardo da Vinci's *The Last Supper* is considered one of the greatest masterpieces of the Renaissance.

As he had promised the duke, Leonardo applied himself in many fields. He designed a device that allowed people to study the total eclipse of the sun without harming their eyes. He designed the first parachute and a model city with two levels and a series of underground canals. An accomplished musician, Leonardo even invented musical instruments. For example, he designed a mechanical drum and an instrument that combined features of a keyboard and stringed instruments.

Leonardo spent countless hours observing nature, drawing and recording in many notebooks what he saw. He also studied mathematics because he believed it was the foundation of art. One of his famous drawings reveals the results of a formula that was first proposed by Vitruvius. The formula and therefore the drawing reveal that the span of a man's outstretched arms is equal to his height.

Beyond Milan

In 1499, war came to Milan when France captured the city. Seeking safety, Leonardo moved first to Mantua (/man*choo*wuh/) and then to Venice, where he worked as a naval engineer. In 1500 he returned to Florence. Except for a year during which he worked for a powerful military leader, he remained in Florence until 1506.

During this period, Leonardo completed his other most famous painting—and perhaps the most famous portrait in the world—the *Mona Lisa*. The painting portrays the wife of a prominent

Florentine citizen. Even today, viewers are attracted by the artist's use of light and shade, his attention to detail in the woman's clothing, and his use of an invented landscape as background. Viewers over the centuries have also been fascinated by the woman's gaze and smile. What was she thinking? People still ask that question as they file past the painting now displayed in the great Louvre (/loov/) Museum in Paris.

Some people say that the *Mona Lisa* is so lifelike that her eyes seem to follow a viewer across a room.

Eventually, Leonardo returned to Milan. He continued his artistic work there, but he also continued to pursue scientific interests. When Leo X became pope, Leonardo moved to Rome, where Leo provided him with lodgings and pay. Later, at the invitation of King Francis I, Leonardo left for France, to become the painter, engineer, and architect of the king. There he remained until his death in 1519 at the age of sixty-seven.

Leonardo left behind relatively few finished works of art: only about a dozen paintings and not one complete sculpture. He did leave many detailed and highly accurate drawings of human anatomy and of various mechanical devices. He also left more than five thousand pages from his notebooks.

Leonardo may not have been the best painter, sculptor, engineer, or thinker of his time. But no one then, and perhaps no one since, has so effectively combined the skills of each calling. No one was more able to imagine what could be. He was in many ways the **embodiment** of the Renaissance, a true **Renaissance man**, devoted to knowledge and beauty in all its forms. Like so much else, the idea of seeking excellence in many fields was borrowed from the ancient Romans. The Romans admired people with all-around ability. They would certainly have admired Leonardo da Vinci.

> ## Vocabulary
>
> **embodiment**, n.
> a person who represents or provides a good example of an idea
>
> **Renaissance man**, n.
> a person who has wide interests, knowledge, and skills

Chapter 7
Michelangelo

Staring at the Ceiling For four years the artist labored, often under difficult conditions. Lying on his back on a platform he had built, he slowly covered the ceiling's five thousand square feet with scenes from the Bible. His patron was not pleased with the pace of his work.

The Big Question

What does the art that Michelangelo created tell us about the Roman Catholic Church at this time in history?

In fact, one day the patron angrily whacked the artist with a cane and threatened to throw him off the platform if he did not work faster.

The artist had not even wanted to accept this job. He thought of himself as a sculptor, not a painter. But the money was very good, and his patron—the pope—was not a man to be denied. So Michelangelo continued to labor on.

It took him four years to complete his work. But when he had finished, the demanding patron, Pope Julius II, was thrilled. The artist, Michelangelo Buonarroti (/bwoh*nahr*roe*tee/), had created a work

LIBICA

This picture shows just a small portion of Michelangelo's painting on the ceiling of the Sistine Chapel.

of magnificence. It was clear that the ceiling of the Sistine (/sis*teen/) Chapel in Rome stood as one of the finest masterpieces of the Renaissance.

Michelangelo was a master of many artistic abilities. He often protested that he was a sculptor, as if he could not be expected to succeed in any other artistic field. In fact, he was a marvelous painter, as you have read. He was also an architect who changed the face of Rome.

Like Leonardo da Vinci, Michelangelo was born near Florence, twenty-three years after Leonardo entered the world. And like Leonardo, he also apprenticed for an artist when he was a boy. In 1488, at the age of thirteen, Michelangelo entered the workshop of a well-known Florentine painter. For one year he learned how to mix paints, prepare backgrounds for paintings, create frescoes, and draw with **precision**. The next year, he accepted an invitation from Lorenzo de' Medici to join a special academy. There he studied the Medici's rich collection of Greek and Roman statues and learned sculpture techniques. He worked and studied with all the artists and humanist thinkers that Medici had gathered around him.

> **Vocabulary**
> ....
> **precision,** n. the use of great care and skill

To Rome

Four years after Lorenzo de' Medici's death, Michelangelo moved to Rome. Like so many artists before him, he was fascinated by the ancient city's sculpture, architecture, and painting. He created

Many people consider this statue of the *Pieta* as Michelangelo's greatest sculpture. Every year millions of visitors to St. Peter's in Rome admire this work.

his first major work in Rome. This established his reputation as a master sculptor. He was then commissioned to create a large marble statue of Mary, the mother of Jesus, holding her dead son.

Michelangelo's extraordinarily lifelike sculpture, called the *Pieta* (/pee*ay*tah/), was said to be the most beautiful work of marble in all of Rome. It remains in that city today. Each year, millions of visitors to St. Peter's Basilica marvel at this magnificent sculpture.

The now-famous sculptor returned to Florence in 1501. There, Michelangelo created a second masterpiece from an enormous block of marble. The block had been left unused for years. Other sculptors worried that the marble had flaws that made it fragile. Michelangelo, however, accepted the challenge. Working for more than two years, he created an awe-inspiring statue of the young biblical hero David, who killed the giant Goliath. The statue seems as if it could be alive. This work confirmed Michelangelo's place as the greatest sculptor of his age.

Four years later, Michelangelo was called back to Rome by Pope Julius II. Julius II wanted the artist to design and build a three-story tomb for the pope's burial. Thus began a strange love-hate relationship between the master artist and the demanding pope. In fact, Michelangelo never completed the tomb as planned. Time and again, Julius interrupted the artist with other jobs.

The Sistine Chapel

One of these interruptions was the assignment to paint the ceiling of the Sistine Chapel, of which you read earlier. Many papal ceremonies were held in this chapel. It was a large project. The artist

The Sistine Chapel is a huge space that took nearly four years to paint.

designed the platform, prepared the ceiling to be plastered—his work was to be a fresco—and hired assistants. In time, he dismissed the assistants because he was dissatisfied with their work.

Michelangelo worked under harsh conditions. When he climbed down from the platform at the end of a day's work, his back and neck ached. His eyes were so used to focusing on a ceiling several feet away that he could not read a letter unless he held it at the same distance.

Michelangelo's finished work was, as you have read, a masterpiece. The frescoes included more than three hundred figures from the Old Testament, some of them 18 feet high. The work covered an area 118 feet long and 46 feet wide. In fact, the Sistine Chapel ceiling would become Michelangelo's most famous work.

After Pope Julius died, Michelangelo stayed on in Rome under the new pope, Leo X. He had known Leo X as the son of Lorenzo de' Medici in Florence. The artist continued work on the statues planned for Pope Julius's tomb. They included a statue of Moses holding the tablets of the law known as the Ten Commandments. The statue is found today in Rome's Church of St. Peter in Chains.

Michelangelo's fresco on the ceiling of the Sistine Chapel shows the biblical story of the creation of Adam.

The statue of Moses holding the Ten Commandments was commissioned as a part of Pope Julius's tomb.

Return to Florence

In 1517, Michelangelo returned once again
to Florence. The pope had asked him
to design the front of the Medici family
church there. There were many problems
with this project. Michelangelo not only had to train new workers
to **quarry** the marble, but he also had to have a road built
through the mountains to transport it. In time, the pope withdrew
the commission. The artist had wasted three years of work and
was furious.

Nevertheless, when a new pope, Clement VII, was elected,
Michelangelo agreed to stay in Florence and design the tombs of
both Lorenzo de' Medici and his brother Giuliano (/joo*lyah*noe/).

Michelangelo's painting, *The Last Judgment,* graces the wall behind the altar at the
Sistine Chapel.

He also agreed to design a library to be attached to the Medici church. His work was interrupted in 1527 when the troops of the Holy Roman Emperor invaded Italy and sacked Rome. With Florence also in danger of attack, Michelangelo fled to Venice.

Eventually, the crisis passed, and Michelangelo returned to Florence. He again took up his work on the library and tomb. In time, a new pope, Paul III, named Michelangelo the chief painter, sculptor, and architect of the Vatican. He also asked the artist to paint a wall behind the altar of the Sistine Chapel. As the theme for this painting, the pope chose the Last Judgment.

Last Judgment and Last Project

Michelangelo began the work, but it took him five years to complete it. He was sixty-six when he finished. The strain of the work affected his health. Once, he fell off a platform, seriously injuring his leg. In spite of these troubles, Michelangelo's genius shines through. *The Last Judgment* is a work of great power.

In 1546, Pope Paul III appointed Michelangelo, then seventy-one years old, chief architect for St. Peter's Basilica. His responsibilities included work on the exterior of the building as well as its dome, which became a model for domes throughout the Western world.

The artist continued working almost until the day he died in 1564.

Michelangelo was buried in Florence as he had wished. Michelangelo, who never married, left no children. He is said to have stated that his wife was his art, and his children were the works he left behind.

Chapter 8
Two "How-to" Men

Instructors in Manners In the Renaissance, as today, people had access to a lot of advice about how to live and act. Today, many articles in print and online claim to teach readers how to succeed in life. Such information was also available during the Renaissance.

> **The Big Question**
> ....
> Why might people have been shocked by Machiavelli's book *The Prince*?

The author of the *Book of Manners* advised people not to gobble their food.

For example, a book titled *Book of Manners* was published in 1558. This title offered readers lots of advice about what kind of behavior was acceptable and unacceptable.

In the *Book of Manners,* the author advises:

- Refrain as far as possible from making noises that grate upon the ear, such as grinding or sucking your teeth.
- It is not polite to scratch yourself when you are seated at the table.
- We should … be careful not to gobble our food so greedily as to cause ourselves to get hiccups or commit some other unpleasantness.
- You should neither comb your hair nor wash your hands in the presence of others—except for washing the hands before going in to a meal—such things are done in the bathroom and not in public.

The purpose of this and other books was to instruct the newly rich about behavior that would help them enter a higher social class. But there was another type of book that had a broader purpose. These books were meant to shape attitudes and to encourage a variety of achievements and to define the role of a gentleman.

> **Vocabulary**
>
> **courtier,** n. a person who serves as a friend or adviser to a ruler in his or her court

The most famous and influential of these books was *The Courtier,* written by Baldassare Castiglione (/bahl*dahs*sah*ray/kahs*tee*lyoe*nah/). A **courtier** (/kor*chyur/) was an attendant in the court of a ruler.

That is exactly what Castiglione was. He served as a soldier and **diplomat** in the court of the duke of Urbino (/ur*bee*noe/).

By the time Castiglione joined the court at Urbino early in the 1500s, the hill town in central Italy had become known as a center of culture. The duke's court boasted one of the finest libraries of the time. A number

Raphael's portrait gives the impression that Castiglione would be an ideal courtier.

of important artists, including the great painter Raphael, worked there. In fact, Raphael painted a wonderful portrait of Castiglione, which now hangs in the Louvre Museum in Paris.

How to Please Others

Castiglione's book was written as a series of conversations that supposedly took place at the court of Urbino. The conversations focused on how men and women could be proper gentlemen and ladies.

The perfect courtier, according to the discussion, should be of noble birth. He should also be handsome, graceful, strong, and courageous. He should be skilled in war and in sports. Whatever he did, he should do it in such a way that it appeared to be without effort.

The courtier, Castiglione and his friends decided, should have a high opinion of his own worth. He should not be afraid to advertise this view to others. But he should not appear to be boastful. So, for example, a courtier should ride near the front in a crowd of people to make sure he would be seen. He should try to accomplish his most daring feats when the ruler he served would notice him.

The ideal courtier, according to Castiglione, should also be accomplished in learning. He should love painting, sculpture, music, and architecture, and be able to sing and dance gracefully.

Castiglione published his book in 1528. In a short time, it was translated into French and English. For many years, it greatly influenced standards of behavior and education in Italy and also in France and England.

Today, it might seem as if the ideal courtier of Renaissance Italy was all style and no substance. But Castiglione argued that by developing the qualities he described, the ideal courtier would encourage his princely ruler to turn to him for advice. By giving good advice, the courtier could exercise great influence in matters of government.

How to Rule

Another important Renaissance writer took a very different view. His name was Niccolo Machiavelli (/nee*koe*loe/ mahk*e*uh*vel*ee/). He lived at the same time that Castiglione served in the court at Urbino. Like Castiglione, Machiavelli served as a diplomat. From 1498 until 1512, Machiavelli held a number of positions

Machiavelli wrote a guide for rulers who wanted to create a lasting government.

in the Florentine government. Each allowed him to observe how government worked or did not work. He was interested in how rulers gained and kept power.

Machiavelli was put in charge of the forces that were to defend Florence against armies headed by Pope Julius II. The pope was angry that Florence had refused to help him expel French troops from Italy. He wanted to put an end to the Florentine republic and restore the Medici family's rule.

Machiavelli's troops could not defend their city. The pope's forces took Florence, and the Medici family was returned to power. Machiavelli lost his government position. He was exiled to a small farm outside Florence.

Advice for the Prince

During his exile he wrote a small book about how rulers ruled. If artists of the Renaissance drew their inspiration from the natural world, Machiavelli drew his from politics. He looked at what happened in the actual world of power and government. He did not write about the ideal behavior of a leader but about the actual behavior of present and past leaders. He called this book *The Prince*. Many think of it as the first book of modern **political science**.

The Medici family was suspicious of Machiavelli. They knew that he really wanted to see Florence ruled by a republican government. Nevertheless, they did employ him again. Soon after, however, the family lost control of Florence, and Machiavelli was once again unemployed. Then he became sick and died, but *The Prince* had caused a stir and had wide influence.

The Prince was not Machiavelli's only work. He also wrote a history of Florence and other political texts. *The Prince*, however, represented, to some extent, new thinking. Because Machiavelli made no attempt to describe politics in terms of religion, he shocked many. But he also described the workings of government very clearly. Rulers took notice.

Machiavelli agreed that, in general, it was praiseworthy for a prince to be faithful and honest. But he stated that a ruler's behavior might need to change in times of trouble or danger. There might be times when a prince would need to act boldly.

And for the safety and well-being of a city or nation, a prince might also need to break a promise, or go back on his word. So for this reason Machiavelli advised princes who wished to gain and maintain power "to learn how *not* to be good."

Like Castiglione, Machiavelli believed that appearances were important. A prince, he wrote, should be seen as merciful and sincere. Machiavelli also wrote that rulers sometimes had to use **cunning**, trickery, even cruelty to achieve a goal, which usually meant staying in power. Over the years many people have strongly disagreed with Machiavelli's advice. In fact, the term *Machiavellian* is still used to describe a person who is crafty and less than honest.

> **Vocabulary**
>
> **cunning,** n. the use of deception or shrewdness in dealing with others

On the other hand, many scholars believe Machiavelli was being realistic. They instead suggest that instead of writing a description of how an ideal ruler should behave, Machiavelli simply offered an honest description of how efficient rulers did behave.

Chapter 9
The Renaissance in Northern Europe

Spread of Spirit and Ideas Both
The Courtier and *The Prince*, we have
seen, had influence well beyond
Italy. Both books were translated into
other languages. Both found readers
in countries throughout Europe.

The Big Question
....
How did the ideas
of the Renaissance
spread to other parts
of Europe?

Translation of the printed word was just one of many ways in which
the ideas and values of the Renaissance spread from Italy to the
rest of Europe.

Italian artists also carried the spirit and ideas of the Renaissance to
other countries. Leonardo, for example, spent his final years in France
as a painter, engineer, and architect to King Francis I. Other Italian
artists of the Renaissance also worked outside Italy, sharing their
skills and ideals.

Visitors to Renaissance Italy often carried home the ideas and
attitudes that were common there. Some visitors, such as Erasmus,
came for learning. They found inspiration in Italy and gladly shared
it with citizens of their home countries. Others, such as the invading

King Francis I of France helped bring Renaissance ideas out of Italy and into the rest of Europe.

German and French armies, came to conquer and steal. In many cases they were influenced by the cultural riches they found. They too carried their discoveries back home, along with their loot.

Several factors made Italy the center of the Renaissance in the 1300s and 1400s: the closeness of Roman ruins, the geography and growing wealth of the independent city-states, the rise of

Europe in the Time of the Renaissance

The influence of Renaissance Italy spread to the nation states of northern and western Europe in the 1500s.

merchants and patrons, and the reform of education. Several factors came together elsewhere in the 1500s to open other countries to new learning and new ideas.

Northern and Western Europe

In the 1500s some countries to the north and west of Italy developed well-organized central governments. The center of trade shifted from the Mediterranean to the Atlantic, bringing some of these countries new wealth. Royal courts in France, England, and Germany supported young artists. New wealth also supported a thriving merchant class. The merchant class became patrons of the arts and learning.

The German-speaking countries of the Holy Roman Empire to the north of Italy were among the first to welcome Renaissance ideals. Men like Erasmus helped spread humanism in those countries. However, the German-speaking regions were soon caught up in religious disputes between Catholics and Protestants. These disputes were part of a movement called the Reformation. Nevertheless, the spread of the Renaissance to the north produced a number of important scholars and artists.

Perhaps the greatest German painter of this period was Albrecht Dürer (/ahl*brekt/du*rur/), born in 1471. His **goldsmith** father took him to his workshop to teach him the trade. But Dürer's father soon discovered that his son had a remarkable talent for drawing. He sent Albrecht to a local artist to work as an apprentice. There young Dürer quickly

> **Vocabulary**
>
> **goldsmith**, n. a craftsperson who makes items out of gold

mastered the technique of **engraving**. Engravings were images carved onto wood or metal plates with a sharp tool. The plates were then inked for printing.

After he finished his apprenticeship, Dürer traveled to France. There he improved the engraving skills he had learned. Dürer was to do some of his finest work as an engraver. He also produced beautiful **woodcuts**. These are prints made by cutting images into a flat block of wood. This flat surface is then covered with ink and pressed onto paper or some other material, leaving an image behind.

Dürer eventually traveled to Italy. He visited Venice, where he discovered new artistic styles. These new forms of expression were different from anything he had known in his native country. While in Venice, he copied the paintings of well-known artists to improve his technique. He also studied

Dürer's engraving, *Melancholia*, was created in 1514.

mathematics, read poetry, and carefully observed the landscapes and life that surrounded him.

After Dürer returned to Germany, he established his own workshop. He soon became popular as a painter and engraver. Two of his most remarkable works were self-portraits.

Dürer created many other portraits, including one of Erasmus. But he was

Dürer's self-portrait shows a young man who is sure of his ability as an artist.

especially interested in engravings and woodcuts. Among his best works of this type is a series of engravings based on the Christian New Testament.

The Renaissance in France

The Renaissance flourished in France in the middle of the 1500s. French invasions of Italy introduced French leaders to Renaissance culture. What they saw amazed them. Earlier you read about how King Francis I hired Leonardo da Vinci to come to Paris. Francis and the kings who followed him purchased many Italian Renaissance paintings and sculptures. They also brought Italian Renaissance artists to France.

The Chateau Chenonceau (/shen*on*soe/) is located in France on the Cher River.

French monarchs also built lavish **chateaux** (/sha*toez/), designed by Italian architects. These rich homes were decorated in the Renaissance style.

The influence of the Italian Renaissance did not stop there. Life in the chateau was modeled on life in Italian courts, as described by Castiglione in *The Courier*.

The Renaissance in England

In England the Renaissance reached its height in the late 1500s and early 1600s. In many European countries it was the sculptors, painters, and architects who made the greatest contributions to the Renaissance. In England it was the writers.

During this period a number of notable poets and playwrights wrote works that are still read, performed, and loved today. Among them was William Shakespeare, often called the greatest playwright of all time. Shakespeare was born in Stratford-upon-Avon in 1564. As a young man, he moved to London. There he established himself as both a playwright and a poet.

There is no record that Shakespeare ever visited Italy. But the influence of Italy and the Italian Renaissance is seen in a great many of his plays. *The Merchant of Venice* is set in the Italian city-state. *Othello* is a tragedy about a Venetian general. *Romeo and Juliet* takes place in Verona. Many of Shakespeare's plots were taken from famous Italian stories.

As you have read, Shakespeare also shared the Renaissance interest in classical Greece and Rome. He wrote several plays about ancient Greece and four tragedies about ancient Rome, including *Julius Caesar* and *Antony and Cleopatra*.

Even when he was not writing about Renaissance

Many of Shakespeare's works were first performed at the Globe Theater.

Italy or the classical world, Shakespeare thought and wrote like a man of the Renaissance. While the Renaissance painters used paint and canvas or plaster to capture ideas and personality, Shakespeare's tools were pen and paper.

The Renaissance in Spain

Compared to other parts of Europe, the Renaissance came to Spain late. Spain's greatest Renaissance painter was actually a Greek, born on the isle of Crete and trained in Venice. His name was Domenikos Theotokopoulos (/doe*men*ih*koes/tha*oe*toe*koe*poo*loes/). After he moved to Spain in about 1577, he became known simply as El Greco—Spanish for "the Greek."

Before moving to Spain, El Greco spent about twelve years in Venice. There, he learned to paint in the Italian Renaissance manner. He was clearly influenced by the paintings of Titian, as shown by the rich colors of his own paintings.

From Venice, El Greco traveled to Rome, where his outspokenness did not win him many friends. El Greco learned a lot from artists in Rome, including Michelangelo. But he offended people by criticizing Michelangelo's paintings. When El Greco saw that he was no longer welcome in Rome, he moved on to the Spanish city of Toledo (/tuh*laid*oe/). El Greco spent the rest of his life in Spain. He was hired to make many paintings, including for churches and chapels. Among his most famous works is a painting known as *The Burial of the Count of Orgaz*. The painting displays the long, slender figures that came to distinguish El Greco's work.

The Burial of the Count of Orgaz includes many characteristics that distinguish El Greco's work.

A Great Writer

Renaissance Spain also produced one of history's greatest writers: Miguel de Cervantes (/mee*gel/de/sur*van*teez/). His best-known work is the novel *The History of Don Quixote de la Mancha* (/dahn*kee*hoet*ay/de/la/mahn*chah/). The hero, Don Quixote, has a noble heart. But he does many foolish things as he tries to imitate the brave knights he has read about. Don Quixote insists that a simple peasant girl he loves is really a noble duchess. He jousts against windmills, thinking they are evil giants. Today, we use the word *quixotic* (/kwihks*aht*ihk/) to describe someone who is impractical or who is striving for an unreachable ideal.

The phrase "tilting at windmills," describing a noble but impractical plan, comes from a scene in *Don Quixote* depicted here.

European Renaissance

As we have seen, the Renaissance began in Italy. It was in Italy that the main features of the period first developed: an enthusiasm for the classical past, an interest in accurately portraying the natural world, a fascination with human beings, and an appreciation for artists and their work.

From the Italian city-states of Florence, Venice, and Rome, the spirit of the Renaissance spread to other countries. But far from simply imitating what had been done in Italy, artists and scholars in other countries developed their own individual styles. What had been done in Italy inspired them to enrich their own local and national traditions. Western civilization benefited greatly from their work.

Glossary

A

apothecary, n. a person who prepares and sells medicines (16)

apprentice, n. a person who trains for a job or skill by working under the supervision and guidance of an expert in the field (52)

B

baptistery, n. a part of a church used for carrying out the purifying ritual of baptism (17)

basilica, n. a type of large Christian church, often built in the shape of a cross (36)

C

cardinal, n. a high-ranking religious leader in the Catholic Church (31)

chateau, n. a French castle, or large country house; chateaux is the plural form (82)

chief of state, n. the recognized leader of a country (45)

"classical literature," (phrase), the works of ancient Greek and Roman writers (2)

commerce, n. the buying and selling of goods and services (8)

commission, v. to formally ask for the creation of something, as in a building or a painting (18)

council, n. a group of people who meet to help enforce laws and run a government (45)

courtier, n. a person who serves as a friend or adviser to a ruler in his or her court (70)

cunning, n. the use of deception or shrewdness in dealing with others (75)

D

devise, v. to come up with an idea, plan, or invention (11)

diplomacy, n. the tactful management of relationships between two or more parties or countries (10)

diplomat, n. a person who represents a government in its relationships with other governments (71)

E

embodiment, n. a person who represents or provides a good example of an idea (57)

engraving, n. an image made by carving a block of wood or metal surface, which is then covered with ink and pressed onto some other surface (80)

exile, n. the state of being made to live outside of a place as a form of punishment (31)

F

form, n. the shape of something (17)

fresco, n. a type of painting made on wet plaster (35)

furnishings, n. the things found in a room, including furniture, rugs, curtains, and artwork (42)

G

galley, n. a flat-bottomed boat with both sails and oars (43)

goldsmith, n. a craftsperson who makes items out of gold (79)

H

hereditary, adj. describing something that is passed down as from a parent to a child (45)

heritage, n. something that is inherited by one person or group from an older person or group (24)

humanist, n. a person who studies or teaches the humanities, that is, literature, history, poetry, and the art of speaking (4)

I

indulgence, n. the removal or reduction of certain punishments for sin, linked to a special act of penance (37)

J

"jack-of-all-trades," (idiom), a person who can do a large number of jobs or tasks (50)

L

lagoon, n. a small body of water that is connected to a larger one (42)

M

manuscript, n. a book or document written by hand (5)

mason, n. a person who builds or works with brick or stone (16)

masterpiece, n. a work of art that demonstrates the highest degree of skill (54)

"merchant class," (phrase), a social class made up of wealthy and powerful merchants (24)

O

oration, n. a public speech (4)

P

papal, adj. having to do with the pope (34)

patron, n. a person who gives money or other support to someone, such as an artist (24)

perspective, n. a technique used to make something that is flat appear to have depth, in addition to height and width (20)

political science, n. the study of how governments work (74)

precision, n. the use of great care and skill (60)

prior, n. a priest who helps lead a monastery (53)

Q

quarry, v. to take stone from the earth (66)

R

realism, n. the quality of being realistic, or true to life (19)

Renaissance man, n. a person who has wide interests, knowledge, and skills (57)

résumé, n. a listing of a person's skills, training, and achievements (50)

revenue, n. income (27)

rhetoric, n. the skill of using words effectively in speaking or writing (5)

S

scholar, n. a person who specializes in a specific academic subject; an expert (2)

senate, n. a group of people who make laws and help govern a place (45)

stable, adj. unlikely to go through changes (22)

T

textile, n. cloth or fabric (42)

three-dimensional, adj. describing an object that has depth as well as width and height, especially a painting that appears not to be flat (20)

V

visionary, n. a person who is able to imagine and plan for the future (50)

W

woodcut, n. a print made by carving an image into a block of wood, which is then used to print the image onto some other surface (80)

The Reformation

Table of Contents

Reader

Core Knowledge History and Geography™

Chapter 1
An Age of Change

Changing Ideas in Europe The world is always changing. Borders grow smaller and bigger. Nations rise and fall. Ideas are accepted and rejected. There has never been an age without change. But at some points in history, things change in especially meaningful or dramatic ways. The 1400s and 1500s were one such age.

The Big Question

What were the obvious advantages of the development of the printing press?

Over the course of the 1400s and 1500s, Europeans developed new ways of communicating. They also formed new ideas about science and religion. These changes transformed European life.

Many people helped transform Europe during these centuries of great change. Seven in particular stand out. They came from countries all across Europe—Germany, Switzerland, France, Spain, Poland, and Italy. One was an inventor. Two had studied **theology**, and two were priests. Two were **astronomers**. With the exception of the Swiss

Vocabulary

theology, n. a system of religious beliefs

astronomer, n. a scientist who studies the stars, the planets, and other features of outer space

Exploration and contact with different cultures brought about huge changes in Europe in the 1400s and 1500s.

and one of the Germans, there is no record that these men ever met each other. In fact, they weren't all alive at the same time. However, all seven of these great people influenced each other as well as our lives today. By studying their lives and work, we can learn about the changes they helped to trigger.

The German Inventor

Johannes Gutenberg (/goo*ten*berg/) created a new technology that would change the way people communicated and, ultimately, the way they thought. Born in Mainz (/mynts/), Germany, about 1400, Gutenberg was trained as a metalworker. In the 1430s he moved to Strasbourg, where he worked cutting gems, making mirrors, and teaching students. Even then, he was probably at work on the invention that would change the world.

By the late 1440s, Gutenberg had returned to Mainz. There he entered into a partnership with two other men.

In medieval times, monks in monasteries copied books by hand because there was no such thing as a printing press.

One was a businessperson. The other was a **calligrapher**, whose job was hand-copying books.

Vocabulary

calligrapher, n. a person who copies written text by hand in an artistic way

Until that time, people in Europe reproduced books by copying them by hand. The process was slow and expensive. Imagine how long it would take you to carefully copy the small book you are reading.

In Gutenberg's time, it might require a professional copyist four or five months of steady work to copy a two-hundred-page text. As a result, only the clergy and the wealthy could afford books. The clergy could depend on monks in monasteries to do the copying required. Wealthy nobles and merchants could afford to pay professional copyists to do the work. At the time, most people did not know how to read, much less own a book.

There was another way to produce copies of a book, but it was too expensive and required painstaking work. Woodcarvers first drew outlines of pictures and words on wood blocks. Next, they followed the outlines to carve out the wood around the letters and images. As a result, the letters and pictures "stood out" on the surface of the block. Then, workers applied ink to each block and pressed the block onto paper.

It was difficult and expensive to make a good printed book this way. Once carved, the words and pictures could not be changed. A single mistake could ruin an entire block. The impressions made on paper were often uneven. Wooden blocks did not last very long and wore down.

People in Europe did not know it, but in East Asia, inventors had developed something called **movable type**. These were small blocks that included a single letter or character. Printers arranged the movable type to create words and sentences. The Chinese created the first movable type out of baked clay in the

eleventh century. By the thirteenth century, Korean printers were using metal to make type. However, movable type did not become popular in China or Korea. Chinese is written using a different character for each word. A printer would have needed to create thousands of pieces of type in order to print a single book.

The Spread of Knowledge

What Gutenberg did transformed the way in which books were produced in Europe. His invention also changed how people communicated knowledge and opinions. Books—and, therefore, knowledge—became available to many more people.

Gutenberg combined two separate developments to reproduce books quickly and cheaply. One development was movable metal type. The other was the wooden screw-and-lever press.

First, Gutenberg manufactured separate letter stamps out of durable metal. He created molds in the shape of each letter. He then poured molten metal into the molds.

How to Make Type

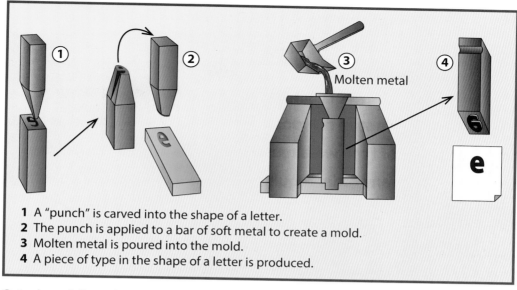

Molten metal

1 A "punch" is carved into the shape of a letter.
2 The punch is applied to a bar of soft metal to create a mold.
3 Molten metal is poured into the mold.
4 A piece of type in the shape of a letter is produced.

Gutenberg followed a multistep process to create his lead type.

Gutenberg repeated this process several times until he had a large collection of lead type for that letter. Then he went on to the next letter. He had to follow the same steps for each letter of the alphabet, including lowercase and capital letters. He also had to make type for numbers and punctuation marks. And he did this for each size of type: small, medium, and large. All in all, he created thousands of different pieces of type.

The lead type pieces were placed in an organizer with lots of little boxes called a type case.

Working With Movable Type

When the time came to print, the printer took the type pieces, letter by letter, from a case. The printer arranged the letters, numbers, and punctuation marks of each line of text in the correct order, with proper spacing, in a strip of wood called a composing stick. Because the metal pieces of type were reusable and because they could be moved around in any order required, they were called movable type.

Next, the printer locked the lines of type into a rectangular frame. Finally, the printer inked the type in the frame and pressed a sheet of paper against it. The printer could then make many prints of the same page. When printing was done, the printer could take apart the frame and return each piece of type to its place in the type case.

Why did movable type become much more popular in Europe than in East Asia, where it had first been invented? Most European languages use twenty-six letters to create words in their language. Written Chinese, which was used across East Asia, used separate characters for each word. It is much easier to create and use twenty-six different pieces of type than thousands. Movable print transformed book production in Europe in ways that would have been difficult in East Asia.

The Printing Press

Gutenberg's second great development was using a wooden screw-and-lever press for printing. The press had been used to make paper or wine. It used a lever and a screw to apply pressure to paper pulp or grapes. The German inventor adjusted the press to print words on paper. First, Gutenberg locked the type onto the

By 1500, most European cities had printers' workshops.

press bed. Then, he applied an oil-based ink to the type by hand and fixed a piece of paper on top of the type. He lowered the screw so that its flat wooden surface pressed the paper against the type and transferred the ink to the paper.

Printing a single sheet took Gutenberg and other early printers about two minutes. It had taken much longer to copy a page of text by hand.

About 1455, Gutenberg created the first printed copies of the Bible. These copies became known as the Gutenberg Bible. The few copies that remain are worth millions of dollars each.

Gutenberg's techniques spread throughout Europe during the next fifty years. By 1500, most European cities had printers' workshops. Printing changed the way information was gathered, stored, and communicated. It greatly increased the number of copies of books and hugely reduced the number of hours required to produce them. Many more people were able to read greater varieties of books, and readers in various places could view the same texts and images at the same time.

Next you will learn how the work of printers helped spread religious and scientific ideas throughout Europe.

Chapter 2
The Birth of Protestantism

Bold Statements It was the eve of All Saints' Day, October 31, 1517. A short, sturdy man strode toward the Castle Church in the German town of Wittenberg. Under his arm he carried a **notice** for display in a public place.

The man had written a series of bold statements on the notice. This notice is now known as the Ninety-five **Theses**.

Vocabulary

notice, n. a written statement posted for the public to see

thesis, n. an idea or opinion; *theses* is the plural form

Martin Luther and his proposed reforms helped begin the Protestant Reformation.

When he arrived at the church door, the man took the notice from under his arm. Then, he fastened it firmly to the door. Anyone who was interested could see what he had written. He did not know how people would respond to his ideas about the Church, but he was certain that he was right. He could not know that his words would start a movement that would change the Catholic Church and all of Europe. By posting his notice containing opinions critical of the Church, the man had begun what would be known as the Protestant Reformation.

In 1517, Martin Luther attached a copy of his Ninety-five Theses, or ideas, to the door of the church in Wittenberg, Germany. These theses explained many of Luther's religious ideas.

This man was a professor named Martin Luther. He was born about forty years after Johannes Gutenberg created his printing press. Gutenberg's press would play a big role in the spread of Luther's ideas.

The German Theologian

In 1483, Martin Luther was born to Hans and Margaret Luther in Saxony, in present-day Germany. Martin's father was a miner who managed to save his money and purchase several mines of his own. Hans Luther was ambitious for his son. He hoped Martin would become a lawyer.

Martin Luther went to school and then to a university. However, at the age of twenty-one he abandoned his studies. Instead, he entered a monastery. Martin Luther's decision angered his father, but the young man believed that he was answering a call from heaven. He was convinced that he needed to become a monk to save his soul. Two years after he joined the monastery, Luther was **ordained** as a priest.

Luther fasted, prayed into the night, and confessed his sins frequently. There were times when those around him thought that he was too stern and too serious. But the leaders of the monastery also recognized his great intelligence. In 1508, he was sent to study to become a **theologian** and four years later became a professor of Bible studies.

While Luther was a student, he was sent on a trip to Rome by his monastery. Rome disappointed him. The lavish palaces of the Church's **cardinals** offended him. He was greatly upset by stories he heard about the pope. It seemed like the pope

Martin Luther was very serious about his studies.

acted more like a ruler of a kingdom than the leader of the Church. Luther thought that many of the people of Rome, including his fellow priests, had little concern for their religion.

A Teacher and Scholar

Professor Luther soon distinguished himself as a teacher. He lectured on the books of the Bible and published writings on religion.

At the time that Luther began his career as a professor, the Church was not only the provider of spiritual guidance, it was also a large international power that required a great deal of management. The Church, led by the pope, ruled a large part of Italy called the Papal States. The pope had an army, waged wars with other rulers, and made treaties. The Church had its own laws and its own courts to deal with Church-related problems. The Church consulted with bankers for financial advice.

Sometimes the Church's political role kept it from performing its religious duties. And, because the Church had grown so much, it constantly needed to raise money to support itself and to carry out its spiritual work. The Church raised taxes, just as taxes are raised today. From time to time, the Church looked for other ways to raise money. For a while, the Church required anyone who held an important Church office to pay the pope part of his salary. The Church also raised voluntary donations given occasionally by a repentant sinner after the receipt of an **indulgence**. An indulgence was a kind of religious pardon from sin or wrongdoing.

> ## Vocabulary
>
> **indulgence,** n. the removal or reduction of certain punishments for sin, linked to a particular act

Challenging Church Practices

When you studied the Renaissance, you learned about indulgences. The Church taught that sins, or mistakes, could keep people from going to heaven. If people sinned, they asked for forgiveness. A priest forgave them and asked them to do **penance**. This meant they did something

Pope Leo X was the son of Lorenzo de' Medici.

to make up for their mistake. The Church also taught that indulgences could release people from part of their penance. But—and this was important—the indulgence would not work unless people also **confessed** their misdeeds to a priest and had been forgiven for having sinned. Sometimes when priests gave indulgences, people in return donated money to the Church. Usually donors were promised a reduction in the number of years their soul would have to spend in **purgatory**.

In 1514, Pope Leo X extended the practice of indulgences across Europe. This increased the Church's ability to raise money.

Vocabulary

penance, n. an act, such as praying, done to show regret over some wrongdoing

confess, v. to admit having done something wrong

purgatory, n. according to Roman Catholicism, a temporary place where the souls of the dead suffer in order to do penance for sins before going to heaven

Luther had studied the Bible. He was convinced that the Church misled people by offering indulgences. He agreed with the Church that God would forgive sins only if people were truly sorry. But Luther thought that receiving donations caused confusion. He believed it gave people the false idea that they could give money in return for God's forgiveness. God's forgiveness, he believed, was not something that anyone could buy.

In April 1517, a traveling monk arrived in Wittenberg, where Luther taught. He was a super-salesman. He told people that they could earn indulgences by giving money for rebuilding the pope's **basilica** in Rome. He said the indulgences he was offering were very powerful. They could even help people's dead relatives gain release from purgatory. The monk made his wild claims because he wanted to raise money for the Church. But everything he said went against Church teachings.

Luther was furious. He summarized on a notice his

This is the door on which Martin Luther nailed his Ninety-five Theses in Wittenberg. Luther was not the first to attack the practices and teachings of the Catholic Church. In fact, over time the Church had put in place a number of reforms. Now, however, complaints such as Luther's could reach a wider audience because of the printing press.

ideas about why the Church was wrong to exchange indulgences for donations. His notice listed ninety-five theses for debate by students at the university. The door of Wittenberg's Castle Church was a kind of bulletin board for university announcements. In October 1517, Luther nailed the notice to the door.

People often nailed notices to the door of this church. But Luther's notice was very dramatic. He objected to how the Church raised and spent money. He denied that the pope had any power over the souls of the dead. And he charged that offering indulgences actually harmed people by making them think that all they had to do was give money and their sins would be forgiven. These ideas were a real challenge to the authority of the Church.

Spreading Luther's Ideas

Luther's theses were printed and distributed throughout central Europe. It is not clear what role Luther played in this process, but he surely allowed it to happen. Luther also began to publish leaflets and pamphlets. In them he explained his views on indulgences and other Church practices. Many people read his ideas.

Church authorities were not happy with Luther's writings. Many thought he was a **heretic**. Church leaders called Luther to a meeting to discuss and debate his writings. When Luther was told he must take back

> **Vocabulary**
>
> **heretic,** n. a person who does not accept or follow the ideas of a particular religion

what he had written, he refused. Luther made it clear that if certain reforms did not happen, then he and his supporters would disobey the Church.

During the next three years, Luther continued to print writings calling for reform of the Church. In his writings, Luther began to question the authority of the pope. He also blamed the pope for many of the Church's problems and attacked some of the Church's teachings. Luther taught that only some of the Church's rituals, called **sacraments**, were based on the Bible. He thought that marriage should not be one of the sacraments. He argued his views with other leaders in the Church. Over time, Luther gained the support of many of the German people.

Finally, the pope took strong action. He issued an official document, called a **papal bull**, in which he condemned Luther's writings and ordered them burned. The pope gave Luther sixty days to take back what he taught or face **excommunication**, or removal from membership in the Church. Luther responded by burning a copy of the papal bull.

> **Vocabulary**
>
> **sacrament**, n. an important Christian religious ceremony
>
> **papal bull**, n. a major and formal written statement from the pope
>
> **excommunication**, n. a punishment given by a high-ranking religious official saying that a person can no longer be part of the Church

Luther on Trial

Luther was ordered to appear before an assembly of religious leaders and princes, including the Holy Roman Emperor Charles V. Luther faced a choice: He could say he was wrong or be thrown out of the Church. The assembly, called a diet, was held in the city of Worms. The people in that city were overwhelmingly in favor of Luther.

Martin Luther (standing, center) defended his ideas at the Diet of Worms.

At the assembly, Luther was shown twenty of the books he had written and was asked if he would **recant** what he had written. Luther refused. "My conscience," he said, "is captive to the Word of God. I will not recant anything, for to go against **conscience** is neither right nor safe." A month later, Charles V agreed that Luther would now be declared an outlaw. Luther fled and hid in the castle of one of his supporters. He remained hidden for almost a year. While in hiding, he translated the entire New Testament of the Bible from the original Greek into German. Now more people could read the Bible.

Luther's translation of the Bible was the best and most readable German version.

Unlike earlier reformers, Luther was now outside the Church, but he continued to demand Church reform. Luther believed that certain Church reforms should be in the hands of local regions or communities who understood the problems. This idea appealed to those in positions of power. More local control meant less interference by the Church. Among his supporters were some German princes, and in particular the Duke of Saxony, who took it upon himself to protect Luther. Without the duke's support, Luther may very well not have survived. Luther's reforms were put into practice in many areas of Germany and in neighboring countries. This new movement was called Lutheranism.

The Holy Roman Empire responded by first allowing Lutheranism in certain areas in 1526 and then banning it in 1529. The followers of Luther and others who disagreed with Rome protested against the new ban. These protestors became known as Protestants. The reform movement Luther began is called the Protestant Reformation. Today *Protestant* means a member of one of the churches that separated from the Catholic Church during the Reformation.

Luther continued to preach and write until his death in 1546. He spoke directly to the people in their own language. Many who heard him joined him in creating a new church independent from the Catholic Church. Today, Luther's followers live in many countries throughout the world. The church they belong to is called the Lutheran Church. It is important to understand though, that when Luther began his protests, he did not intend to start a new church. His original aim was to reform the Catholic Church.

Chapter 3
The Spread of Protestantism

A Second Wave of Religious Reformation Switzerland is southwest of Luther's Germany. This mountainous country's geography encouraged independence among its citizens. The rugged Alps made it difficult for others to conquer the Swiss.

The Big Question

Besides Lutheranism, what other Protestant religions developed in Europe?

In the early 1500s, Switzerland was divided into many smaller territories called cantons. Each canton governed itself. In the late 1200s, a number of cantons formed a **confederacy** to help protect themselves against enemies.

Vocabulary

confederacy, n. a group of people, organizations, or countries that join together for a common cause

It was here, in Switzerland, where the second wave of religious reformation took place. In the early 1500s, most of the Swiss bishops were more like feudal lords than spiritual leaders. They often showed greater interest in raising money than in saving souls.

The second wave of religious reform started in Switzerland.

More Religious Reform

What were considered abuses in the Church angered one Swiss citizen in particular, Ulrich Zwingli. Zwingli served as a priest in Zurich, then the leading city in the Swiss Confederation. In 1519, Zwingli began to reform his own congregation. He had become convinced that many practices in the Church had no basis in **scripture**. Like Luther, he opposed the practice of indulgences. He urged people not to seek them. "Christ alone saves," he declared.

He also preached against other practices he said were not supported in the Bible. He dismissed the **veneration** of the **saints**. He ordered all statues and other forms of religious art be removed from churches. He declared that Christians were not required to fast or go on **pilgrimages**. Since he could not find authority in the Bible for the use of music in worship services, he removed the organ from his church and banned the singing of hymns. Zwingli won many supporters in Zurich.

Thanks to the help of a supportive Zurich printer, Zwingli's ideas were spread outside Zurich. Copies of his **sermons** and other writings reached Germany. There Zwingli's ideas began to compete with Martin Luther's.

> ## Vocabulary
>
> **scripture,** n. religious writings; the Bible
>
> **veneration,** n. the act of showing honor or deep love or respect
>
> **saint,** n. a person honored by religious leaders for having lived an especially good and exemplary life
>
> **pilgrimage,** n. a journey undertaken for religious purpose
>
> **sermon,** n. a speech on a religious topic given by a religious leader

Luther and Zwingli Meet

The two reformers did not always get along. First, they carried out a pamphlet war. Then, in 1529 they met in person to debate their differences. They agreed on many teachings. Both agreed that religious beliefs and practices should be based solely on what was in the Bible. This differed from the Catholic view, which was that the traditions handed down from the earliest days of the Church were important, too. But the two reformers differed strongly on the role of the Church in people's lives. At the end of their meeting, Zwingli offered to shake hands with Luther. Luther flatly refused. "I will not let the devil teach me anything in my church," he later said.

Zwingli returned to Zurich, where he continued to write and preach. His teachings were not supported by some cantons of Switzerland that still followed the Catholic faith. In 1531, five of these cantons **mustered** an army against Zurich. Zwingli joined the Zurich army as a **chaplain**. The Swiss reformer was killed in battle. As he lay dying, he is reported to have said, "They may kill the body, but not the soul."

> **Vocabulary**
>
> **muster,** v. to gather soldiers together
>
> **chaplain,** n. a religious person who serves a specific group, such as an army or a hospital

Despite Zwingli's death, the spirit of religious reform remained alive in Switzerland. It shifted, however, to another Swiss city, Geneva. In Zurich, German was the common language. In Geneva, located close to France, most people spoke French. It was a

The Swiss reformer, Ulrich Zwingli (left), and the French reformer, John Calvin, both influenced the Protestant revolution.

Frenchman who would bring the message of reform to Geneva and ensure its spread to many other parts of Europe.

The French Scholar

John Calvin was born in 1509 in northern France. He studied theology and philosophy in Paris and planned to become a priest.

In the middle of his studies, his father sent him to another city, Orleans, to study law. Calvin completed his legal studies, but he never practiced law. While in Orleans, he began to read the writings of religious reformers. He even began to spend time with some of them.

In about 1533, Calvin experienced what he called a "sudden **conversion**." Within a year he began to support Protestantism openly.

> **Vocabulary**
>
> **conversion,** n. the act of changing from one religion or belief to another

In Catholic France, people who wanted to reform the Catholic Church were not welcome. So Calvin moved from France to Basel, Switzerland.

Calvinism

While in Basel, Calvin wrote a book called *The Institutes of the Christian Religion.* In the *Institutes* Calvin discussed his views on religious belief and practice. The first edition of the *Institutes* was published in Latin. Two years later it was published in French.

One of the most important theological issues of the time was the question of God's forgiveness of sin or wrongdoing and who would or would not receive **salvation**. The Catholic Church taught that sinners needed to ask God's forgiveness for their sins and do penance to receive salvation. Luther said that it was really only God's forgiveness that was important. Calvin, however, believed that God *chose* who received salvation. According to Calvin, God decided who would receive salvation and who would not—and that God made this decision about a person before he or she was even born. This idea is known as ***predestination***. Some people, Calvin believed, were predestined to go to heaven; others were not.

> **Vocabulary**
>
> **salvation,** n. in Christianity, being saved from the effects of sin
>
> **predestination,** n. the idea that a person's actions and fate are decided ahead of time by God

Calvin also wrote about the relationship between Church and state. He maintained that the authority of **civil** rulers is based on God's word. Lawful civil rulers, he said, acted as "officials and lieutenants of God." Therefore, he believed that the word or laws of God were above all others.

Vocabulary

civil, adj. related to the government, not to religious or military organizations

In 1536, Calvin moved from Basel to Geneva. There, other reformers persuaded him to help turn the wealthy independent city into a center of religious reform.

A Calvinist Government

Calvin and other reformers wanted to create a government in Geneva that would put his beliefs into practice. Calvin taught the people of Geneva the beliefs he wrote about in the *Institutes*. He also attempted to make belief in his teachings a requirement for anyone who wanted to remain a citizen of Geneva. Calvin also attempted to control the behavior of the people of Geneva. He restricted activities such as gambling, singing, dancing, and drinking. The reformers wanted good citizens to watch over their fellow citizens' behavior and report any crimes. Those who continued to behave "badly" would be excommunicated.

At first, Geneva officials rejected Calvin's system. They exiled him and his fellow reformers. But three years later they called him back. Only Calvin, they decided, could reverse the increase in

While Calvin won followers in Geneva, leaders there forced him to leave the city for a time.

"bad" behavior they saw in Geneva. The officials also worried that if he did not return, Catholicism would return to Geneva.

Calvin drew up a new set of rules for Geneva. The new laws were based on the Bible. A group of **pastors** would decide how to worship, and they would oversee the behavior of every resident of Geneva.

Calvin also started an academy to train ministers. His students traveled throughout Europe and carried his teachings to France, the Netherlands, England, and Scotland. In France and

England, Calvinism had success, and in the Netherlands and Scotland, Calvinism eventually became the main form of religion.

In Switzerland and the Netherlands, followers of Calvin called themselves the *Reformed Church*. In Scotland, they became known as *Presbyterians*. The name referred to the Church's form of government, in which **elders,**

Dominant Churches and Religions in Europe (Mid-1500s)

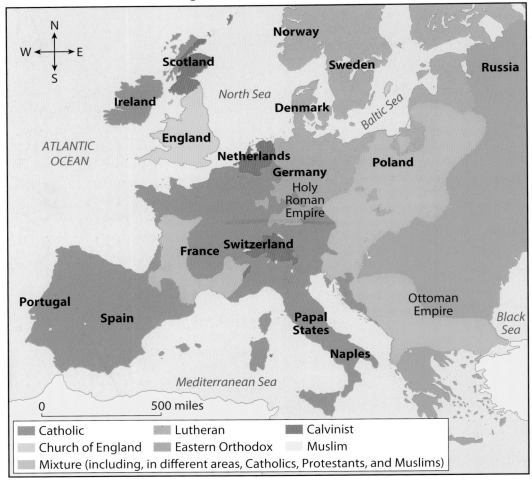

By the mid-1500s, different religious groups dominated different countries and regions in Europe. Jewish people also lived in many parts of the continent.

or presbyters, played important roles. Immigrants and merchants from the Netherlands and Scotland helped spread Calvinism to other parts of the world.

Henry VIII

In England, Henry VIII rebelled against the Catholic Church for personal—not religious—reasons. Henry's rebellion was not Calvinist or Lutheran. Henry was a Catholic whom the pope had declared "Defender of the Faith" for his opposition to Luther.

Later, though, Henry decided he no longer wanted to be married to his wife Catherine. He asked the pope to **annul** the marriage. The couple had a daughter, Mary, but they did not have a son, which Henry needed as an **heir** to the English throne. Henry wanted the pope to declare that his marriage should not have been allowed because Catherine had once been married to his older brother Arthur. Arthur had died at a young age. When the pope refused to grant the annulment, Henry rebelled. Henry

appointed his own Church leaders, who granted him a divorce. Henry then married a woman named Anne Boleyn (/boe*lin/). The Church excommunicated Henry. After all of this, Henry and Anne would have a daughter, Elizabeth, but not a son.

King Henry VIII of England established a new church when the pope refused to allow the annulment of his marriage.

Henry decided to establish the Church of England, with himself as head. The new Church of England, or Anglican Church, broke all ties with Rome. Although Henry had broken with Rome, the new English Church was not as radically Protestant as Calvinist churches.

There were some Englishmen who thought the English Church had not been reformed enough and remained too much like the old Catholic Church. These people, known as Puritans, were heavily influenced by Calvin's thinking. In the early 1600s, many of these Puritans would sail to New England, in North America.

Chapter 4
A Revolution in Science

Changing Scientific Ideas While Catholics and Protestants debated religion, scientific ideas were also changing. Gutenberg's printing press made it possible to quickly spread new information and thinking about the Earth, the heavens, and the human body far and wide.

New scientific ideas and discoveries from this era would bring great changes to our understanding of the world in which we live.

> **The Big Question**
> ....
> How might scientific discovery have challenged religious belief?

Comète de Donati
— Ptolémée observant les astres —

The ancients observed the heavens. They watched what happened in the night sky and tried to make sense of the patterns they saw.

The Polish Astronomer

In 1473, Nicholas Copernicus was born to a leading Polish merchant family. Young Nicholas received an excellent education. He studied first at the University of Krakow, where he became interested in mathematics and astronomy. Then he received further training at two universities in Italy.

By the time he came home to northern Poland, Copernicus had mastered almost all the learning of his day. From his uncle, a bishop, Copernicus received a Church position that paid him an income for the rest of his life. Holding this office required him to become a priest. Copernicus remained a loyal Catholic until his death.

The Church was very interested in problems of astronomy in the 1500s. It had realized that the calendar—designed by Julius Caesar and called the Julian calendar—was inaccurate. Christians were not correctly calculating the date of a major holiday called **Easter**. Scholars had to study the movements of the sun and planets in order to determine more accurately the length of the year.

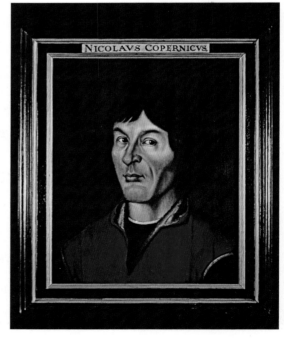

Nicholas Copernicus was a Polish astronomer who taught that Earth and other planets in our solar system revolved around the sun.

Since ancient times, almost everyone had agreed that Earth stood still at the center of the universe. As he worked on this problem, Copernicus grew dissatisfied with the common understanding of the universe.

In the 100s CE, the Greek astronomer Ptolemy (/tol*uh*me/) had used mathematics to describe how the sun, moon, planets, and stars circled Earth. However, Copernicus did not agree with Ptolemy's view that Earth was immovable. He learned that in ancient times, not all Greeks shared Ptolemy's thinking. Some had **theorized** that the sun stood at the center of the universe and that Earth, as well as other planets and stars, moved around it. Perhaps, Copernicus thought, these theories could help explain how the heavens appeared to rotate around Earth every year. But there were problems.

> **Vocabulary**
>
> **theorize,** v. to come up with an idea explaining some complex event or thought

It seemed impossible that Earth rotated around the sun—wouldn't it just spin off into space? Also, the scientific wisdom that Europeans had inherited from ancient Greece was that Earth was solid whereas the heavens were light and fiery. How could something as heavy as Earth be moving?

Some of Copernicus's concerns were related to religion. The Bible said that God had once made the sun stand still. Wasn't it wrong to say that Earth moved and the sun didn't? Also, what if Earth turned out to be just one more planet circling the sun? Could Earth still be the center of God's creation?

These concerns didn't stop Copernicus. He concluded that Ptolemy was wrong. He decided "to read again the works of all the philosophers" in order to find a better answer.

Copernicus lived after the invention of Gutenberg's printing press. Because of it, the Polish astronomer was able to examine far more records and references than any astronomer before him. He did not have to travel to distant libraries to read and copy manuscripts written by Islamic and European scholars. Instead, printed texts were available to him in Poland.

The Observations of Copernicus

Copernicus studied the stars and reviewed what others had written about them, He became convinced that it was Earth that moved and that the sun remained still. He also concluded that Earth moved in

Vocabulary

axis, n. an imaginary straight line around which a spinning object rotates

two ways. First, it spun on its own **axis**, making one full rotation every twenty-four hours. Second, Earth and the other planets revolved around the sun. For Earth, this journey took one year. In Copernicus's view, then, the sun was the center of its own system within a larger universe.

Although Copernicus came to these conclusions early in the 1500s, he would not publish them until many years later. In the

This drawing of the Copernican theory shows the sun in the center of the revolving planets.

128

meantime, he gained fame and respect as an astronomer. He even won the favor of the pope, who approved the diagrams and calculations Copernicus used to explain his theories. In 1536, the Polish scientist was given permission to publish his findings.

Although there were attempts to stop Copernicus, in 1543, *On the Revolution of the Heavenly Bodies* was published. Legend says that a copy of the book was brought to Copernicus on the day he died, May 24, 1543.

Copernicus's work was groundbreaking. But it was just the beginning. His ideas provided a new starting point for astronomers to follow him.

The Italian Scientist

Galileo Galilei was born in Pisa, Italy, in 1564, just twenty-one years after Copernicus had died. He became fascinated with mathematics after a visit to the cathedral church in Pisa in 1583. According to legend, he watched a lamp swinging back and forth at the end of a chain. He observed that no matter how far the lamp swung, each swing seemed to take the same amount of time.

Years later, Galileo followed up his observation by carrying out a series of experiments with all sorts of **pendulums**. He discovered that his observation had been correct. Because of his discovery, he designed an adjustable pendulum that doctors could use to measure the **pulses** of their patients. Later, this discovery

> **Vocabulary**
>
> **pendulum,** n. something hung from a fixed point that swings back and forth as a result of gravity
>
> **pulse,** n. a throbbing feeling caused by the movement of blood in the arteries of the body

provided the basis for the development of the pendulum clock.

Galileo had originally gone to university to study medicine. After a year of study, he began to seriously study mathematics instead. In time, he was invited to teach math at universities, including the University of Padua, where Copernicus had once studied.

Early in his career, Galileo showed great interest in understanding the

Legend says that Galileo experimented by dropping objects from the famous leaning tower of Pisa.

laws that governed the movement of physical objects in space. He disproved the notion, put forward by the ancient Greek philosopher Aristotle, that objects of different weights fall at different speeds. He did this by dropping two objects of unequal weight from different heights. Galileo used experiment and observation to form his own scientific conclusions.

In 1609, Galileo learned of the recent invention of the telescope. In a short time he had built one of his own. His telescope was much stronger than previous models. Galileo began to use it to study astronomy. He had long been convinced that Copernicus's theory of how planets revolved around the sun was accurate.

Using his telescope, he confirmed his belief.

Galileo published his observations in 1610, in a book titled *The Starry Messenger*. Opposition came quickly. Many Catholics and Protestants felt threatened by his work. They believed it was contrary to the Bible. Catholic theologians persuaded the Church's Holy Office to take action against Galileo. The Holy Office was responsible for rooting out heresy in the Church.

Galileo created his own, more powerful telescope to observe the stars and planets.

In 1616, Galileo was called before the Church's chief theologian. Galileo was told that the Church had decided to condemn the ideas of Copernicus, on which so much of Galileo's work was based because they appeared to be at odds with Church teachings. From then on, the writings of Copernicus would be placed on the Index of Forbidden Books. Galileo was told he could not teach that the work of Copernicus was true. He had to teach that the idea that planets revolved around the sun was a theory. Galileo agreed to these terms, knowing that severe penalties, even torture, might follow if he did not. For several years, Galileo worked quietly. He continued his studies without publishing his results. Then, in 1632 he published the greatest of his astronomical writings, the *Dialogue on the Two Chief Systems of the World—Ptolemaic and Copernican*. It was a thorough defense of the Copernican system. It suggested that the ideas of Copernicus were more than a theory. This made those ideas more dangerous to Church teachings.

Galileo wrote his *Dialogue* in Italian rather than Latin so it could reach a wider audience. The Catholic Church reacted quickly. Although Galileo was now an old man, he was ordered to appear in Rome to be tried for heresy.

The Church Condemns Galileo

On June 21, 1633, the Church condemned the *Dialogue*. Galileo was ordered to take back his support for the teachings of Copernicus. After being sentenced to prison, the old scientist was forced to kneel and deny what he believed. Galileo had never stated that the Bible or Church teachings were wrong, but rather there were aspects of the world that were not fully understood. Nevertheless, the Catholic Church felt threatened.

Galileo spent the last eight years of his life under house arrest. He did not publish any books on astronomy. Instead, he wrote about motion and the structure of matter. This provided a basis for modern physics.

In the years following his death in 1642, other scientists continued Galileo's work. In time, many people accepted the Copernican view of the universe. It's important to understand that the Catholic

Church was not against scientific research or understanding.

At this time in history, the Church, and indeed the Bible, were at the heart of European society. The Church in Rome was driven to protect religious teachings and to hold the Church together as one religious body. Eventually, it too would accept the work of Copernicus and Galileo, and several members of the Church would go on to make their own groundbreaking scientific discoveries.

Chapter 5
Reform Within the Church

Reform Within the Catholic Church Many members of the Catholic Church who did not join the Protestant reformers also disagreed with some of its teachings and practices. They too were upset at the behavior of Church leaders who seemed more interested in the material world than in the spiritual good of their people.

The Big Question

What were the outcomes of the Counter-Reformation?

In Spain, efforts to reform the Catholic Church—including the founding of centers of learning such as the Complutense University— helped limit the spread of Reformation ideas.

Instead of leaving the Church, they decided to try to change the Church from within. They hoped they could change the course of the Church while holding to the Catholic faith.

In fact, long before Martin Luther wrote his Ninety-five Theses, Catholics had been concerned about the failures of the Church and had tried to reform it. In some places, such as Spain, reform came from Church leadership. Officials of the Spanish Church grew alarmed at the fact that many priests were not educated enough to do the work the Church expected of them. They were also concerned about the low standards of behavior in many monasteries. As a result, reform followed. The Church also founded the Complutense University, which became a great center of learning. As a result of this work, Lutheranism and Calvinism never firmly took root in Spain.

Elsewhere, such as in Italy, reform was a **grassroots movement**. New monastic groups devoted themselves to spreading religion and serving the poor and the sick. The Oratory of Divine Love was founded for that purpose in the same year that Luther posted his theses. The Franciscan

> **Vocabulary**
> ....
> "grassroots movement," (phrase) a reform movement beginning with and coming from ordinary people

Order of the Capuchins (/kah*poo*chinz/) was organized eleven years later. The group's name came from the *capucini*, or hoods, the members wore. The Capuchins were devoted to teaching and preaching among the poor and to living simple lives. The Ursulines (/er*suh*linz/), an order of women dedicated to teaching girls and caring for the sick and the poor, began in 1535.

The Spanish Priest

One of the most effective of the Catholic reformers was Ignatius (/ig*nay*shus/) of Loyola. He was born in 1491 to a noble family in northern Spain. In 1517, the same year Luther posted his theses, Ignatius became a knight for an influential relative. Later in life he admitted that at that time he was interested mostly in going to war and being a successful soldier.

In 1521 his life changed. During a battle his leg was broken by a cannonball, leaving him unable to walk. While he recovered from his wounds, he asked for books, hoping to read tales of knightly heroes and beautiful ladies. But there were only two books available in the castle where he was recovering; a book on the life of Jesus and a book on the lives of saints. The books moved Ignatius deeply. After much thought he decided to change his life and do penance for his misdeeds.

In 1522, Ignatius made a pilgrimage to a **shrine** dedicated to Mary, the mother of Jesus. There, he hung his sword and dagger near Mary's statue and became a beggar. For nearly a year he prayed and did penance. He also wrote a little book,

> **Vocabulary**
>
> **shrine,** n. a place considered holy because it is associated with a holy person or event

called *The Spiritual Exercises*, as a guide to self-reform. This book would be widely read and followed.

After a pilgrimage to the holy site of Jerusalem, Ignatius became a student. He was in his thirties and was much older than the other students. He forced himself to sit with the younger students and learn the basics of Latin and other subjects. He studied for more than twelve years, first in Spain and then in Paris.

Following this time period, Ignatius became friends with other like-minded people who shared his strong beliefs and devotion to good works. Because of his strong beliefs and

Ignatius was a towering figure of reform in Spain.

his enthusiasm for sharing them, Ignatius often came under suspicion and was even arrested. He was charged with **heresy** ten times, and he was sometimes imprisoned, but each time he was found not guilty.

In 1537, Ignatius and most of his companions were ordained priests and began to preach and work with people. Two years later, in Rome, the companions decided to form a group dedicated to serving the pope in whatever way he commanded. In 1540, Pope Paul III approved the new group. They were given the name the

A Paulus Tertius Pontifex Maximus, anno salutis   B. Constitutiones ac regulam S. Pater, scribit.   C. Filios suos ad praedicandum euangelium in
1540, Societatem Iesu confirmat. lib. 2. 17.   lib. 4. 2.   uarias mundi plagas dimittit. lib. 5.

Ignatius founded the Jesuits with the blessing of Pope Paul III.

Society of Jesus. Ignatius was elected their first leader. In time, the members of the society became known as Jesuits (/jezh*yoo*itz/).

The Jesuits

For the next fifteen years, Ignatius led the Jesuits as they quickly grew. They devoted themselves to preaching, caring for the needy, educating the young, **converting** nonbelievers, and fighting against heresy.

They ran their society like the military, perhaps because of the military experience Ignatius had had as a young man. Society members accepted strict discipline. They gave their leader the title *general,* and they obeyed him without question.

The Jesuits became well-known for their work in education. Ignatius recognized the need for highly educated members of the order, so he established schools to train new members. In time, the value of the Jesuits' training was widely recognized. Jesuits were asked to take over many universities. By 1600, four out of five Jesuits were teachers. Jesuits were also running hundreds of schools and colleges. Within fifty years they were the most important educators of European Catholics.

Council of Trent

Although the Jesuits were leaders in bringing about reform in the Church, they did not do so alone. In fact, the pope who approved their establishment, Pope Paul III, made important contributions of his own. He appointed a group of cardinals to investigate abuses in the Church. He began drastic reforms based on their recommendations. He also demanded that bishops actually live within the community they were supposed to serve. He set up the Roman **Inquisition** to investigate and root out heresy. Most important, he set up the Council of Trent, a meeting of Church leaders, which took place in northern Italy. The Council of Trent sought to examine and clarify the beliefs and practices of the Catholic Church.

> **Vocabulary**
>
> **Inquisition,** n. a court of the Catholic Church that sought to discover and punish anyone who believed or practiced things that were against Catholic teachings

The council began meeting in 1545. It did not finish its work until eighteen years and three popes later. The council hoped

The Council of Trent met in 1545 to consider reforms for the Catholic Church and reaffirm many of the Church's teachings.

to reunite different Christian groups that had developed. However, the division had grown too great. Instead, the council defended and further explained many of the Catholic teachings Protestants had questioned.

Martin Luther and other reformers argued that the Bible alone was the authority for Church teaching. The council said that Church tradition also provided such authority. And it claimed that the Church alone had the right to interpret the Bible.

Luther held that salvation came from faith alone. The council agreed that faith is necessary for salvation. But it declared that believers could help ensure salvation through good works and by taking part in Church sacraments.

Luther, Zwingli, Calvin, and other reformers had attacked the practice of indulgences. The council continued to teach that indulgences granted by the Church granted less time in purgatory. But the council did try to correct abuses involved with indulgences. It also warned against **superstition** in such matters as the worship of the saints.

Like Protestant reformers, Catholic leaders of the Counter-Reformation used printing to spread their message. Printing presses helped Ignatius of Loyola's *Spiritual Exercises* reach a large audience, just as Luther's and Calvin's writings had. Printing presses also allowed the Church to gain greater control over some practices. Printed editions of texts and directions for worship services, for example, were made the same for everyone.

Forbidden Books

The Council of Trent tried to control forces that had been released as a result Gutenberg's invention. Concerned about the accuracy of translating the Bible into different languages, the Catholic Church tried to control the publication of such texts. It established an Index of Forbidden Books. And just as Protestant churches in Protestant regions did, the Catholic Church required writers of religious books to get permission to publish.

The work of people such as Ignatius of Loyola and others helped create a new sense of purpose in the Catholic Church. The work of the Council of Trent helped rid the Church of serious abuses. It emphasized the importance of education, especially the training of its priests and teachers. It confirmed the Church's basic teachings and established a set of rules and practices throughout the Church. In this way the Church survived the Protestant Reformation.

Glossary

A

annul, v. to officially state that a marriage never existed under the law (121)

astronomer, n. a scientist who studies the stars, the planets, and other features of outer space (92)

axis, n. an imaginary straight line around which a spinning object rotates (128)

B

basilica, n. a type of large Christian church, often built in the shape of a cross (106)

C

calligrapher, n. a person who copies written text by hand in an artistic way (95)

cardinal, n. high-ranking religious leader in the Catholic Church (103)

chaplain, n. a religious person who serves a specific group, such as an army or a hospital (115)

civil, adj. related to the government, not to religious or military organizations (118)

confederacy, n. a group of people, organizations, or countries that join together for a common cause (112)

confess, v. to admit having done something wrong (105)

conscience, n. a sense or belief a person has that a certain action is right or wrong (109)

conversion, n. the act of changing from one religion or belief to another (116)

convert, v. to change from one belief or religion to another (139)

E

Easter, n. an important Christian holiday celebrating Jesus Christ's rising from the dead (126)

elder, n. a person who has power and authority based on experience (120)

excommunication, n. a punishment given by a high-ranking religious official saying that a person can no longer be part of the Church (108)

G

"grassroots movement," (phrase), a reform movement beginning with and coming from ordinary people (136)

H

heir, n. a person who will legally receive the property of someone who dies; the person who will become king or queen after the current king or queen dies or steps down (121)

heresy, n. ideas that go against the main teachings of a religion (138)

heretic, n. a person who does not accept or follow the ideas of a particular religion (107)

I

indulgence, n. the removal or reduction of certain punishments for sin, linked to a particular act (104)

Inquisition, n. a court of the Catholic Church that sought to discover and punish anyone who believed or practiced things that were against Catholic teachings (140)

M

movable type, n. a system of blocks for individual letters and punctuation marks that can be arranged to print books and other written documents (96)

muster, v. to gather soldiers together (115)

N

notice, n. a written statement posted for the public to see (100)

O

ordain, v. to officially make a person a religious leader **(103)**

P

papal bull, n. a major and formal written statement from the pope **(108)**

pastor, n. a Christian leader in charge of a church **(119)**

penance, n. an act, such as praying, done to show regret over some wrongdoing **(105)**

pendulum, n. something hung from a fixed point that swings back and forth as a result of gravity **(129)**

pilgrimage, n. a journey undertaken for religious purpose **(114)**

predestination, n. the idea that a person's actions and fate are decided ahead of time by God **(117)**

pulse, n. a throbbing feeling caused by the movement of blood in the arteries of the body **(129)**

purgatory, n. according to Roman Catholicism, a temporary place where the souls of the dead suffer in order to do penance for sins before going to heaven **(105)**

R

recant, v. to publicly take back something you have said or written **(109)**

S

sacrament, n. an important Christian religious ceremony **(108)**

saint, n. a person honored by religious leaders for having lived an especially good and exemplary life **(114)**

salvation, n. in Christianity, being saved from the effects of sin **(117)**

scripture, n. religious writings; the Bible **(114)**

sermon, n. a speech on a religious topic given by a religious leader **(114)**

shrine, n. a place considered holy because it is associated with a holy person or event **(137)**

superstition, n. a false belief in the power of magic, luck, or unseen forces **(142)**

T

theologian, n. an expert on the study of religious ideas **(103)**

theology, n. a system of religious beliefs **(92)**

theorize, v. to come up with an idea explaining some complex event or thought **(127)**

thesis, n. an idea or opinion; *theses* is the plural form **(100)**

V

veneration, n. the act of showing honor or deep love or respect **(114)**

England in the
Golden Age

Table of Contents

Reader
Core Knowledge History and Geography™

Chapter 1
Elizabeth I

Long Live the Queen According to legend, twenty-five-year-old Elizabeth was sitting under an oak tree reading the Greek Bible on the morning of November 17, 1558. She was expecting important news. Maybe she had decided to read outside so that she could hear the hoof beats of a horse as it galloped toward her house in the English countryside.

The Big Question

How did Queen Elizabeth I manage the conflicts between the Catholics and the Protestants?

The horseman arrived shortly before noon that day. He must have bowed as he presented Elizabeth with the ring of Mary Tudor, Elizabeth's older half sister. The ring was proof that Mary was dead. And if Mary was dead, Elizabeth was now queen of England.

Queen Elizabeth I was at Hatfield House when she heard the news of her sister's death.

Elizabeth is said to have closed her book and fallen to her knees. Speaking in Latin, she said, "Time has brought us to this place. This is the Lord's doing, and it is marvelous in our eyes."

A Dress of Gold and a Velvet Cape

Elizabeth certainly knew about time. She had been waiting to become queen for nearly twelve years. First her sickly half brother, Edward VI, ruled. Then her half sister, Mary Tudor, sat on the throne. During these years, Elizabeth had had time to plan.

Within a week of Mary's death, she marched into London with a thousand men and women whom she had chosen as her advisors and servants.

From the beginning, Elizabeth understood that although heredity had put her on the throne, she needed the support of the English people to stay there. A march with a thousand people was a way to show her power.

Elizabeth's **coronation** day, the day she was crowned, was a spectacular event. Ladies of the English court had sent to Belgium for silks and velvets to be made into gowns for the great day. Although years of religious conflict and war had left England deeply in debt, Elizabeth I made sure her coronation would be unforgettable. She wore a dress of gold and a cape of crimson velvet lined with fur. On her head sat a gold crown.

> **Vocabulary**
>
> **coronation,** n. the ceremony or act of crowning a ruler

These clothes were heavy, but they looked like the clothes of a powerful monarch. That was exactly the impression Elizabeth I wanted to give.

Queen Elizabeth I ruled England for almost half a century, raising her kingdom to a peak of glory.

The coronation was a religious ceremony. Elizabeth I wanted to end the conflicts in England between Catholics and Protestants. At her coronation, she was crowned by a bishop, an official of the Catholic Church, but she insisted that the bishop read from an English Bible, the kind used by Protestants, rather than the Latin Bible used by Catholics.

A Dangerous Situation

From the time when Elizabeth was a little girl, her life had been in danger. England was a nation divided by religion. Elizabeth's father, King Henry VIII, had broken from the Catholic Church in 1529 because the pope would not **annul** his marriage to his first wife, Catherine. Henry and Catherine had only one surviving child, Mary, and

> **Vocabulary**
> ....
> **annul,** v. to officially state that a marriage never existed under the law

Henry wanted a son. Henry wanted to be free of Catherine so that he could marry Anne Boleyn, who later became Elizabeth's mother. Despite the pope's refusal to annul the marriage, Henry married Anne anyway and established the Church of England to be independent of the Catholic Church in Rome. Henry proclaimed himself head of the Church of England. However, when Elizabeth was only two years old, her father had her mother executed. Henry promptly married again. His third wife produced a son, Edward.

After King Henry's death, Edward, Elizabeth's younger half brother, reigned from 1447 to 1553. Edward VI supported the Protestant religion and wanted England to become a Protestant

After King Henry VIII died, his son Edward and then his older daughter Mary sat on the throne.

nation. However, he had been a sickly child, and he died at the age of fifteen. Now it was Elizabeth's older half sister's turn to rule. In 1553, Mary Tudor became Queen Mary I. Mary was Catholic. During her five years on the throne, she restored power to the Catholic Church in England and **persecuted** Protestants. Her brutal persecution of Protestants earned her the name "Bloody Mary."

Unlike Mary I, Elizabeth was a Protestant, though she respected many of the Catholic **rituals** and customs. When she took the throne, Elizabeth faced the difficult task of keeping the peace between Catholics and Protestants.

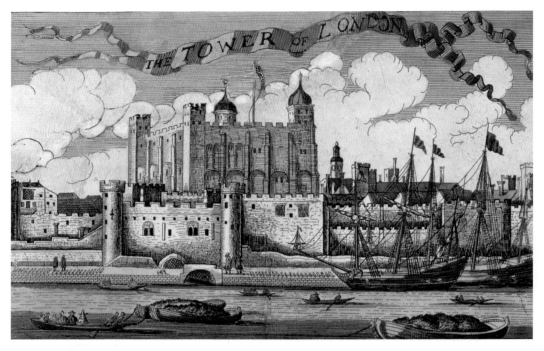

Mary I imprisoned her sister Elizabeth in the Tower of London.

From an early age, Elizabeth learned to pay attention to what was going on around her. She avoided putting in writing any thoughts or beliefs that her enemies might use against her. When Mary I was queen, she imprisoned Elizabeth in the Tower of London. For two months, Elizabeth lived in a cold, drafty cell, never knowing whether or when she might be executed. Queen Mary spared her life, but Elizabeth never forgot the horror of awaiting her own death sentence.

Even after she became queen, Elizabeth I had to be very careful. Another Mary, this one known as Mary Stuart or Mary Queen of Scots, plotted against Elizabeth. Mary, a Scottish queen, was the niece of Henry VIII. She believed that she herself, not Elizabeth, belonged on the throne of England because the Catholic Church did not recognize Henry's marriage to Elizabeth's mother.

Elizabeth's advisors told her to have Mary Queen of Scots put to death. At first Elizabeth was reluctant to execute a relative who was a queen in her own right. Mary was held in **custody** for more than ten years. But when she was finally caught in a plot to have Elizabeth killed, she was brought to trial.

The verdict? Guilty. The punishment? Death.

Queen of Her People, Bride of Her Nation

Throughout the first decades of her reign, Elizabeth's advisors and the **English Parliament** urged her to marry. They wanted her to have a child who could take the throne when she died. They also thought that a woman could not rule as well as a man. Many ambitious men asked for her hand in marriage. Elizabeth argued, however, that marriage would only distract her from her many duties as queen. She considered England to be her husband and her family.

The Queen's Travels

Frequently in summer, Queen Elizabeth I and her court left London on journeys into the countryside. One reason was that she needed to escape from the hot, dirty, and smelly city. London was the largest city in Europe at that time. It had ninety thousand people and no sewers, no running water, and no toilets. Because there was no refrigeration, food spoiled quickly. People did not understand then that unclean conditions spread disease. But they did know that the city was unhealthy in the summer.

The number of people in Queen Elizabeth's court was enough to fill a large village. When her courtiers and their horses arrived at one of the queen's more than sixty castles or houses, they quickly ate all the available food. Although the queen's houses were grand, many were not big enough to fit her whole court. Some of the people who waited on her had to sleep in tents on the grounds. There was no plumbing, sewers, or easy way to dispose of garbage. With so many people in one place, the area quickly became filthy and even unhealthy. People had to clear out so that the area could be cleaned up.

The trip from one residence to another was no small undertaking. Such a trip typically involved hundreds of carts and thousands of packhorses. When Queen Elizabeth I traveled, more than just government officials accompanied her. Cooks, doctors, carpenters, people to sew and do laundry, and people to care for horses also came along. The luggage in the caravan included the queen's clothes and jewels, documents, dishes, linens, equipment, tools, and her massive carved bed.

Even the best and most widely used roads in England were very poor by today's standards. They were dirt roads that turned to mud in wet weather. In dry weather, deep ruts could tip a cart over or break its axle. The caravan of horses and carts could cover only ten or twelve miles a day, roughly the distance that someone might cover on foot.

As Queen Elizabeth I traveled, she sometimes saved money by staying overnight in the houses of different nobles. It was very

PALATIVM REGIVM IN ANGLIÆ REGNO APPELLATVM NONCIVTZ,
Hoc est nusquam simile.

It was not unusual for the journey from one castle to another to last a month. During this time, the queen and her advisors continued to conduct the business of the kingdom.

expensive for an **aristocrat** to feed the queen and her court. Yet, nobles competed for the honor of hosting her. Their power and position depended on her favor. Some aristocrats even added extra rooms to their houses or added buildings to their estates in preparation for their queen's arrival!

Elizabeth's journeys from place to place were also exciting for the common people in her kingdom. She could see how they lived and the state of their towns and farms. The commoners had a chance to see their

queen. People put on plays and **pageants** in her honor. Elizabeth listened patiently to their speeches and once stood in the rain to watch a presentation by schoolboys.

At every opportunity, Queen Elizabeth I told her subjects that she loved them, and she expressed her appreciation for their loyalty. The time she spent traveling did a great deal to increase the people's affection for Elizabeth.

Glorious Reign

Elizabeth combined practices of both the Catholic Church and the Protestant Church when she reestablished the Church of England. Priests wore robes, as in the Catholic Church, but they could marry. The Church services were in English, as Protestants wished. But crucifixes and candles adorned the altars in the style of Catholic cathedrals. Elizabeth I did not persecute Catholics or Protestants for their religion. People who disobeyed her wishes were another matter, however.

Perhaps because of the threats on her life, Elizabeth expected complete loyalty from everyone in her court. Her maids, who were women from noble families, had to get permission from her before they could marry. If one of them married in secret, Elizabeth might imprison the husband until she could be sure that he was not part of a plot against her. Elizabeth demanded loyalty, and she received it.

William Shakespeare, one of the greatest English playwrights, wrote plays to entertain Elizabeth. Composers wrote songs for her to enjoy. Francis Drake sailed around the world for her. She transformed England from a land weakened by conflict into a unified kingdom that could compete with mighty Spain and France for power.

Elizabeth I ruled for forty-five years, from 1558 to 1603. By the time she died, she had given her own name to her era. It was a time of great literature and exploration, but it was not named for William Shakespeare or Sir Francis Drake. We remember it today as the Elizabethan Age.

Chapter 2
Britannia Rules the Waves

Sir Francis Drake Depending on your point of view, Sir Francis Drake was either a hero or a pirate. To English people and to Queen Elizabeth I, he was a brave and skilled sea commander. To the Spanish, however, Drake was a pirate.

The Big Question

Why might the Catholics in England have chosen to be loyal to their Protestant queen, rather than support King Philip of Spain?

During the late 1500s, while Elizabeth I was on the throne, the Spanish were building a great empire. Spanish **galleons** carried gold, silver, precious stones, expensive dyes, and sugar across the ocean from colonies in the Americas. Sir Francis Drake and other English sailors attacked Spanish ships and grabbed some of these riches for themselves.

Vocabulary

galleon, n. a large sailing ship, used as a warship or for trade

Caca Fogo.

Caca Pla

Sir Francis Drake was a hero to the English and a pirate to the Spanish.

The Spanish considered Francis Drake a thief. But a Spanish **nobleman**, whose ship Drake attacked, described him as a great navigator and commander. The same nobleman commented on how well Drake treated his fellow sailors, as well as how much they respected him. Queen Elizabeth I also admired him and showered him with gifts.

Our Golden Knight

Francis Drake left home for the voyage of his life in 1577, a trip around the world! He sailed down the west coast of Africa and then across the Atlantic Ocean and around the Americas. He took every opportunity to attack Spanish and Portuguese ships, and to seize their riches. By the time Drake returned to England three years later, the Spanish **ambassador** to London called him "the master-thief of the unknown world." The following year, however, Queen Elizabeth I **dubbed** him "our golden knight," and he became Sir Francis Drake.

> **Vocabulary**
>
> **nobleman,** n. a person of the upper class; an aristocrat
>
> **ambassador,** n. a person who is an official representative of his or her government in another country
>
> **dub,** v. to officially make someone a knight

To honor their queen and to compete with Spain's mastery of the seas, Englishmen such as Drake explored the world in search of riches. Expeditions set out to establish trade routes across the Pacific Ocean. Walter Raleigh, another of Elizabeth's favorites, tried to start a colony in the Americas. The first Roanoke colony,

Aboard Drake's ship *Golden Hind*, Elizabeth I touched a sword to Francis Drake, making him a knight.

on an island off the coast of North Carolina, did not last. Most of the colonists returned home in a few months. A second group disappeared a short while later. Decades would pass before the English succeeded in establishing a permanent colony in North America.

The Invincible Armada

Even though their colonies had not succeeded, the English still annoyed the Spanish. Spain had claimed North America as its own. It had colonies in Mexico and in the areas of the

United States now known as Florida, California, New Mexico, Texas, and Arizona. In addition to England's colonizing efforts, Drake and other Englishmen continued to attack Spanish ships and seize their treasure. There was more than these things, however, behind the tension between the two countries. Just before Queen Elizabeth I had Mary Queen of Scots executed, Mary had named the Spanish king, Philip II, as successor to the English throne. Remember that unlike Elizabeth, Mary and Philip were both Catholic. The pope later offered King Philip "a million in gold" if he would conquer England.

English and Spanish ships engaged in many battles over the years. After Sir Francis Drake led a surprise attack that destroyed ships in a Spanish harbor, Philip began making plans to invade England and finally conquer it.

People heard rumors that Spain was building a fleet of warships called an armada (/ahr* mah* duh/) for an attack on England. Day and night, coast guards peered across the ocean looking for the

> ### Vocabulary
>
> **resin,** n. a sticky substance that comes from trees and can be lit

Spanish fleet. The English placed pans of flammable **resin** on little platforms on hills across the land. If a lookout spotted an invading ship, he would light one of these beacons. As soon as the people guarding the beacons farther inland saw a coastal beacon shining, they would light their beacons. This signaled others farther inland. In this way, news of an invasion would spread quickly through England.

The "invincible" Spanish Armada attempted to invade England in 1588.

Finally, in July 1588, the Spanish fleet was spotted. Dubbed the "Invincible Armada" by the pope because they could not be defeated, the Spanish ships were an impressive sight. The armada had 130 large ships that sailed in a tight formation. They were like floating fortresses. These ships carried more than 30,000 people, as well as horses and weapons. The Spanish were not planning a sea battle. They planned to invade England and capture it with a land battle.

The English fleet, on the other hand, carried only 1,500 men. Their ships were small, but they were nimble. The English sailors also knew all the **currents** of the waters in which they fought. They darted around the edges of the Spanish formation, picking at the outermost ships.

The English set empty ships on fire and let the ocean currents carry them toward the armada. This forced the Spanish ships to break out of their tight formation to avoid the flames. Still, Spain might have conquered England if it had not been for the weather. As the Spanish retreated, a powerful storm blew dozens of their ships onto the rocks of Ireland and Scotland. The ships that survived withdrew to Spain. Nearly half of the men in the Spanish Armada died.

Prayer and Thanksgiving

During Elizabeth's reign, Spain was the greatest sea power in the world. Many English people were truly terrified that Spain would conquer England and make it a Catholic country once again. King Philip of Spain had counted on England's Catholics to rise against their queen and aid his invasion. Instead, the English Catholics stayed loyal to their own government. This gives us some idea of how much progress Queen Elizabeth I had made in healing the religious conflicts in her kingdom. Nonetheless, many people in England used the conflict with Spain as a reason to distrust Catholics.

In November 1588, Elizabeth declared a day of thanksgiving. Everyone was urged to go to church, just as Elizabeth herself did. She thanked God and asked her people to do the same.

Chapter 3
The Civil War

After Elizabeth Queen Elizabeth I lived to be nearly seventy years old. That was a long life for someone in the 1500s—and for someone whom so many people had wanted to kill!

The Big Question

Why did Parliament distrust Charles I and his wife Henrietta?

The legend is that as she lay dying, she whispered to the archbishop of Canterbury the name of her successor to the throne.

Whom do you think she named the next ruler? She named her closest relative, James Stuart, the son of her great enemy, Mary Queen of Scots.

Unlike his mother, however, King James VI of Scotland was a Protestant. In England he was called James I.

King James I

James I believed he ruled by the **divine right of kings**. Like Elizabeth I, King James I wanted to keep Protestants and Catholics at peace with each other. He held a conference in 1604, shortly after he was crowned, to try to bring the two groups together. The only thing they

Vocabulary

"divine right of kings," (phrase), the belief that kings and queens have a God-given right to rule and that rebellion against them is a sin

IACOBVS 6
SCOTOR
ÆTA 3
159

James I became king of England and Scotland after Elizabeth I's death.

agreed on, however, was that a new translation of the Bible was needed. James ordered a new translation. The result was the King James Version, also known as the King James Bible. It became one of the most widely read and quoted books in English.

In 1607, a group of English colonists settled in Virginia and named their colony Jamestown, after King James I. The Jamestown settlers endured many hardships. They finally succeeded in establishing the first permanent English colony in North America.

Around this same time, two groups of Protestants in England were unhappy with the Church of England. One group, called the Separatists, wanted to separate entirely from the Church of England. The other group decided they wanted to worship in a simpler way that they felt was truer to the faith of the Bible. They were called Puritans because they wanted to "purify" the Church of England.

In 1620 a group of 103 Separatists sailed to North America to create a colony. They settled in Plymouth, Massachusetts. We remember them today as the Pilgrims. In 1630, English Puritans, the people who wanted to change or "purify" the Church of England, settled in what is now Boston, Massachusetts. They built towns throughout "New England." They generally lived in plain and simple ways. Puritans frowned on such pastimes as dancing and gambling. They also did not wear fancy clothes or jewelry.

When King James I died in 1625, his son, Charles I, took the throne.

The English Separatists who settled in Plymouth, Massachusetts, became known as Pilgrims.

Trouble All Around

Charles I was a weak, sickly child. He did not walk until he was seven years old. Like his father, James I, and Queen Elizabeth I before him, he believed that he had been chosen by God to rule. Unlike Elizabeth, however, Charles did not understand that he needed the support of his people to stay on the throne.

Charles I was devoted to the Church of England. But he chose Henrietta Maria, the Catholic daughter of the king of France, as his wife. As monarchs did back then, Charles married to form an **alliance** with another powerful country. The idea was that, if the king married a French princess, the two countries would be less likely to go to war against each other.

Vocabulary

alliance, n. an agreement between nations in which they work together toward a common goal or fight on the same side in a war

Charles I married France's Princess Henrietta. Because Henrietta was Catholic, her presence created conflict in England.

The French Catholic princess brought a large group of priests and other French Catholics to wait on her. When some members of the English government found out, they were furious. Within a year, King Charles was forced to send a bishop, 29 priests, and 410 of the queen's attendants back to France.

The king or queen of England was the head of the Church of England, unlike the Catholic Church whose head was the pope. The Church of England, however, still kept many of the rituals of the Catholic Church in its church services. As we have seen, some Protestants, such as the Separatists and Puritans, did not like this.

By now the Puritans had become a more powerful group. In fact, many of the men in the English Parliament were Puritans or agreed with Puritan ideas. In Scotland, which was also part of Charles's kingdom, Protestants who wanted to remove Catholic influences from the Church of England were called Presbyterians. Puritans and Presbyterians were suspicious of Charles, his Catholic wife, and their love of religious rituals and symbols.

A Prayer Book and a Civil War

Worried about the growing power of the Puritans, King Charles ordered Presbyterians in Scotland to start using a prayer book based on the one used in the Church of England. His order angered some people, and riots broke out. When Charles refused to take back his order, a Scottish army marched into England.

The English Parliament distrusted King Charles so much that it had not given him money for an army for many years. The army that he sent to fight the Scots in 1639 was unpaid and poorly equipped. The English soldiers ran away from the enemy. Charles asked members of Parliament again for money. Because he was so unpopular, they responded by having two of his most important **officials** arrested.

Charles then marched to Parliament with three hundred soldiers to arrest the ringleaders of what had become a rebellion. The men he was looking for had escaped.

> **Vocabulary**
>
> **official,** n. a person who carries out a government duty

"I see the birds have flown," said Charles, and it was clear now that he had few, if any, supporters in Parliament. London was in an uproar. King Charles realized that it was not safe for him to stay in the capital city. In 1642 he escaped to northern England to raise an army to fight his own Parliament.

Roundheads and Cavaliers

Like most **civil wars**, this one was painful and confusing. Families were divided, with some members supporting the king and others supporting Parliament. Some were loyal to the king even though they thought he was at fault.

In general, nobles who had **country estates** supported the king. Many of the people who worked on these estates supported the king as well, either out of loyalty to their landowners or because they were afraid to take another position. The Royalists, those who supported the king, were also called Cavaliers. The word comes from the Spanish world *caballero*, which means horseman or cavalry. Cavaliers were given that name

A Cavalier (left) and a Roundhead (right)

by those who opposed them. Those people shouted "cavalier" at the well-dressed, aggressive young nobles who strutted in the streets of London. Today we might describe someone who seems arrogant and thoughtless as cavalier.

Most people who lived in London and other large towns supported Parliament. These people were known as Roundheads because they favored the short, simple haircuts of Puritans.

Soldiers on both sides lived in crowded, dirty conditions that allowed the spread of deadly diseases. These diseases sometimes spread to nearby towns and killed people who were not even fighting in the war. Soldiers also demanded taxes, food, and livestock from the villages that they marched through on their way to battle. All in all, the war brought suffering to everyone, even those who tried to stay out of it. By the end, about one in five people in England had been killed by the war or the diseases it brought.

Chapter 4
The Puritan Ruler

The End of the War The English Civil War dragged on for four years. One reason it lasted so long was that neither side really knew what it was doing. In those days, England had no standing army—that is, it had no permanent troops ready to go to war at a moment's notice. Most of the men fighting on both sides were poorly trained.

The Big Question

Why might Oliver Cromwell have once earned the reputation of being a dictator?

The few professional soldiers in the country fought on the side of the king. Even the commanders had very little experience on the battlefield. Yet there was one commander on Parliament's side who had a talent for leadership. That man was Oliver Cromwell.

Young Oliver Cromwell

Oliver Cromwell was born four years before the death of Queen Elizabeth I. His family belonged to the class of people called the gentry. Members of the **gentry** were a level lower than nobles on the social ladder.

Vocabulary

gentry, n. people who own land and have high social standing but no titles of nobility

Oliver Cromwell commanded Parliament's troops during the English Civil War.

One of Cromwell's ancestors had been a high-ranking advisor to King Henry VIII, Queen Elizabeth's father. When Henry broke away from the Catholic Church, he took land away from the monasteries in England and gave it to his friends. Cromwell's family received a large grant of land at that time.

Although Cromwell grew up in a Puritan family, it was not until he was nearly thirty that he became deeply religious. After suffering from a series of mysterious illnesses, he had a religious experience and dedicated himself to serving God.

Cromwell in the Civil War

Cromwell was not happy under the rule of Charles I. He did not approve of Charles's sympathy for Catholics. Also, Cromwell was a member of Parliament, which had its own troubles with the king.

When the English Civil War began in 1642, Cromwell pulled together a troop of soldiers and led them to fight against Charles I. As their captain, Cromwell demanded of his men the same qualities he demanded of himself: selfless dedication and strict discipline.

His troops won battle after battle, and Cromwell rose in **rank**. He began to build up Parliament's armies, trying to accept only religious men to serve as soldiers. He thought that belief in God would give them a reason to fight. He did not allow swearing or drunkenness among his troops. He promoted officers according to their performance, not their background or privilege.

Vocabulary

rank, n. a position in a group or organization

178

Cromwell led Parliament's army to victory in the English Civil War. His troops, nicknamed "Ironsides," never lost a battle.

Parliament used many of Cromwell's ideas to create England's first national army, known as the New Model Army. Before this, quite often different armies had been loyal to individual noblemen, not to the country as a whole. In 1646, the king's Royalist forces surrendered to the New Model Army. Parliament had won the war.

However, once Parliament no longer had to fight the king, many disagreements broke out among its members. Now what would Parliament do?

Treason!

Charles I believed that God meant for him to rule. The fact that the Cavaliers had lost to the Roundheads was not important to him. Charles tried to use the disagreements among the members of Parliament, the New Model Army, and the Scots to regain power for himself. He made a secret deal with the Scots, promising to share power with them if he could regain the throne. A second, shorter civil war soon began. Cromwell once again defeated the king and his supporters.

After the short, second civil war, Cromwell and other leaders of the army decided to put Charles I on trial for **treason**. This was a shocking idea. That a king, chosen by God to rule a country, could betray that country and be tried for treason was not acceptable to many. Members of Parliament, even those who had supported the civil wars, objected. The army, however, was stronger than Parliament. Soldiers stood outside the courtroom, stopping members of Parliament who opposed the trial from entering.

> **Vocabulary**
>
> **treason,** n. the crime of being disloyal to one's own country

King Charles I was tried for treason and convicted. He was sentenced to death.

The trial of Charles I lasted five days. At the end, Charles was condemned as "a Tyrant, Traitor, Murderer, and Public Enemy," to be "put to death. . . ."

The Ax Falls

The execution of Charles took place on a cold day at the end of January 1649. Thousands of people came to see the shocking sight of a king executed by his own people. In 1649, it probably seemed unbelievable to them that such a thing could happen.

Charles put on two shirts so that he would not shiver and cause people to think that he was afraid to die. Even in the face of death, however, he did not change his views. He declared again that the common people should not share in government but be ruled from above by their king. According to Charles, God chose kings. As the king was executed, one person watching said, "There was such a groan by the thousands then present, as I have never heard before, and desire I may never hear again."

Lord Protector

Parliament wanted Cromwell to become the king, but he refused. If he had accepted, the army probably would have turned against him. Instead of continuing as a **monarchy**, England, Scotland, Wales, and Ireland essentially became a **republic**.

The army made Cromwell the head of the nation. His title was Lord Protector. Although he was not a king, he governed like one. His new government passed laws that reflected Puritan views. These laws dictated what people could or could not do on Sundays. There were also harsher punishments for swearing, gambling, and drunkenness. These laws, however, were not strictly enforced.

> **Vocabulary**
>
> **monarchy,** n. a government led by a king or queen
>
> **republic,** n. a government in which people elect representatives to rule for them
>
> **"public policy,"** (phrase) laws or rules, both written and unwritten, that govern society

In his personal life, Cromwell was not as strict as he was in his **public policies**, nor was he as strict as many of his followers. Cromwell did however impose very harsh policies against Catholics in Ireland. Thousands of men, women, and children died at the hands of his soldiers. Cromwell took away land from Irish Catholics and gave it to

English landowners. But in England, Catholics and followers of other faiths had a greater degree of religious freedom.

Throughout his five years as head of the country, he experimented with different forms of government, trying to find one that worked. He got rid of one Parliament and then, two years later, he created a new one, which he later **dissolved**. At one point, he appointed eleven major generals to manage different areas of England.

None of the methods that Cromwell tried worked very well. Today, though, historians believe that his willingness to try different things helped move England toward a more democratic system. For about two hundred years after he died, however, history remembered him largely as the man who killed a king and ruled as a **dictator**.

Chapter 5
Merry Monarch and Brother

The Fugitive King Although the Parliamentarians, led by Oliver Cromwell, had executed King Charles I, they had not killed his son, Charles II. The people of Scotland were unhappy that the English had killed Charles I, who was their king, too. They proclaimed Charles II their new king.

The Big Question

Why did many people not want James II to be king?

In 1650, the year after the execution of his father, Charles II led an army of Scots against Cromwell. As usual, Cromwell was victorious. Young Charles, little more than a teenager then, was suddenly on the run from Cromwell's army.

The Parliamentarians offered a large amount of money for the capture of "a tall young man two yards high, with hair deep brown to black." For six weeks, Charles hid in villages and forests until he could arrange for a ship to take him to France. In a short span of time, his life greatly changed from that of the son of a king to that

After his father was executed, Charles II tried to fight Cromwell's army and ended up fleeing to France.

of a **fugitive** hiding in the woods. Many people must have seen him and known who he was, yet no one turned him in.

Charles escaped to France and then, for the next eight years, he wandered around Europe. He had no money and few friends. Cromwell turned the governments of France and Holland against him.

The End of "Sword Rule"

People called the military government of Oliver Cromwell "sword rule." Remember, Cromwell had made the English army stronger than it had ever been. That had allowed the Parliamentarians to defeat the forces of Charles I and the Scots who fought for Charles II. Once the wars were over, however, the army was still strong. The army practically controlled the government, and the English people did not like that.

When Cromwell died in 1658, his son Richard took over, but he was not a strong leader. England seemed to be falling apart. Many in England wanted to return to a government with a king and a Parliament. In 1660, the English Parliament invited Charles II back to England to be king.

The Merry Monarch

Charles II returned to England on May 29, 1660. It was a day of great excitement and rejoicing. People were tired of the strict Puritan laws and the high taxes collected by the army. The return of a monarch was called the **Restoration**.

The excitement over the return of Charles II and the hopes for a stable government led people to regard Charles as a hero for his years in hiding. Paintings and tapestries showed him hiding behind oak trees to escape from Cromwell's soldiers.

Charles, unlike his father, understood that he needed the support of Parliament and of his people to stay on the throne. He said that he had no wish "to go on his travels again." He supported Parliament as it reestablished the Church of England. Many people in England now saw the Church of England as a good **compromise** between what most still viewed as the dangers of the Catholic Church and the strictness of the Puritans. Parliament also **disbanded** the army.

The monarchy was restored, and Charles II was welcomed back as king.

Charles II was called "the Merry Monarch" because he liked to have fun.

Charles was certainly no Puritan. He was known as the Merry Monarch because he loved the kind of pleasures that many Puritans had tried to outlaw during the rule of Cromwell. He liked to gamble and to go to horse races. He also enjoyed attending the theater. Under Charles II, for the first time in England women could appear on the stage as actors. Before that, men and boys played all the women's parts. Charles was known as fun-loving, but many considered him lazy, too!

Parliament Has the Upper Hand

The nation had a king again, but there was no doubt about how the king had arrived. Parliament had invited the king back, and Parliament did not give up all its power when Charles arrived.

Charles would have been happy to allow religious tolerance everywhere. Many people believed that he was a Catholic at heart. In fact, he **converted** to the Catholic religion on his deathbed. During his reign, however, Charles knew that if he admitted that he was Catholic, he would lose his throne.

> ### Vocabulary
> **convert,** v. to change from one belief or religion to another

Charles would have liked to let the English people practice any religion they wished. Parliament, however, was now suspicious of both Catholics and Puritans. Parliament restored the Church of England and made it stronger than ever. Puritans lost their jobs, and their worship services were forbidden. Instead, Puritans, Quakers, and other Protestants who did not belong to the Church of England were called Dissenters. Some of them went to colonies in North America to escape persecution.

Plague, Fire, and Trouble

The laziness of Charles made many people anxious. In some ways, the country seemed to still be falling apart. The kingdom was running out of money. Rivalry over trade routes led to several small wars with Holland. Then, Dutch ships sailed into an English harbor, sank five English ships, and towed a battleship back to Holland. People ridiculed Charles for not paying enough attention to running his kingdom.

During Charles II's rule, two other setbacks occurred. They were not Charles's fault, but they cast a shadow on his reign. One event was an outbreak of the **bubonic plague**. Officials recorded almost one hundred thousand deaths from the plague in London alone in 1665.

Vocabulary

bubonic plague,
n. a deadly disease spread by fleas on infected rodents

The other unfortunate event happened the following year. A baker's oven in a crowded section of London started a fire that burned out of control for four days. The Fire of London destroyed some thirteen thousand houses as well as many important churches. After the fire, about one hundred thousand people were homeless.

The king also faced a problem all too familiar to the English monarchy. Charles II and his queen had no children. The next in line for the throne was James, the brother of Charles. James was a Catholic.

The Great Fire of London raged out of control until Charles II ordered all buildings in its path to be blown up.

James II

In 1685, Charles II died and James became King James II. Although James and Charles had been raised in the Church of England, their mother, Henrietta, had influenced them. Charles II converted to Catholicism on his deathbed. James converted to Catholicism when he was about thirty-five.

James first married a Protestant Englishwoman. They raised their children as Protestants in the Church of England. After his first wife died, however, James married a Catholic princess from Italy.

Although it had been more than a hundred years since a Catholic monarch had ruled England, many English Protestants still feared that a Catholic ruler would persecute Protestants. The English people were afraid of their Catholic ruler, James II.

When the Catholic wife of James became pregnant, people became even more worried. If their unborn child was a boy, a long line of Catholic rulers might begin. Many powerful people in England decided that it was time to rid themselves of this king. To achieve this, seven important leaders in Parliament, known to later admirers as the "Immortal Seven," decided to call in some help from the outside.

Chapter 6
The Glorious Revolution

William and Mary Before the birth of James II's son, the next in line for the throne had been James's older daughter, Mary. Mary was a Protestant; she was married to William of Orange, a hero to Protestants in Europe.

The Big Question

Why was a foreign ruler invited to invade England?

William was a popular Dutch prince and the grandson of King Charles I. He was the major defender of Protestant Holland against the king of France. France had replaced Spain as the most powerful Catholic country in Europe.

In the fall of 1688, the Immortal Seven, the seven important leaders of Parliament, sent an invitation to William. They invited him to bring an army to England. They told him that they would support him. This was a very unusual thing to do. These seven leaders of Parliament were inviting a foreign ruler to invade their country!

William of Orange was married to James II's daughter, Mary. In 1688, leaders of Parliament invited William to invade England.

William's Motives

William of Orange was only too happy to accept this invitation. He wanted England's military power on his side. William feared that France was going to invade Holland.

But William had two major problems. One was that England's Catholic king, James II, was an ally of France. The other problem was that if William sailed into England, France might take his absence from Holland as an opportunity to invade his country.

By pure chance, two events happened that changed history and allowed William to invade England. The first was that the king of France, King Louis XIV, decided to attack a Protestant region of what is now Germany instead of Holland. The second was that the wind shifted. Normally at that time of year, the winds in the **English Channel**

Vocabulary

English Channel, n. a body of water between southern England and northern France that connects the North Sea and the Atlantic Ocean

blew from west to east, making it difficult to sail from Holland to England. In 1688, however, a strong wind rose up that blew from the northeast. That was exactly the wind that William needed to invade England. Called the "Protestant wind," it allowed William to bring his ships quickly across the channel to England.

Once William landed on English soil, many landowners and members of Parliament joined his cause. The queen took her new baby and escaped to France. Because so many Protestant officers in James's army deserted to fight for William, the king panicked

William of Orange led his troops into London without a fight.

and followed his wife and child. William led his troops into London without fighting a single battle.

Everyone was quite surprised. When the Immortal Seven invited William to England, they were hoping only to scare James II. They wanted him to give up the Catholic religion and give more power to Parliament. They were not expecting that he would flee the country!

A King *and* a Queen

Now there was real confusion. William was not in line to take the English throne. His wife, Mary, was the daughter of King James II. Yet William was not willing to rule simply as the companion of the queen.

Many English leaders considered it unacceptable that the throne should pass over Mary, the **heir** to the throne by birth, to a more distant relative. They could think of only one solution. In February 1689, Parliament decided that James II had abandoned the throne when he left England for France. Therefore, Parliament declared that the throne was vacant. Then Parliament offered the crown to William *and* Mary. William would be King William III and Mary would be Queen Mary II. The king and queen would rule together as equals.

An Unusual Coronation

Like many monarchs before them, William and Mary had a grand coronation. Never before, however, had two people received crowns at once. And what crowns they received! It is said that 2,725 diamonds, 71 rubies, 59 sapphires, 40 emeralds, and 1,591 large pearls decorated two gold crowns. The crowns were so heavy that both William and Mary looked tired from the effort of wearing them before the coronation ceremony was over.

There was another way in which the coronation was unusual. Previous rulers had promised to uphold the laws of their ancestors when they were crowned. William and Mary, however, promised to uphold the laws of Parliament. They also agreed to uphold the Protestant religion.

The transfer of power from James II to William and Mary became known as the "Glorious Revolution" or the "Bloodless Revolution". It was an important step toward democracy. Instead of accepting the idea that the choice of a ruler should be based on birth alone, leaders of Parliament chose a ruler based on what they thought was best for the country. The rulers themselves agreed to uphold the laws made by Parliament, not the laws made by previous kings and queens. And the English got rid of a ruler they did not like without resorting to execution.

The Bill of Rights

It was not enough just to choose a new king and queen, however. In 1689, Parliament passed one of the most important acts in the history of England: the English Bill of Rights.

The English Bill of Rights is one of the foundations of the English government. It puts limits on the power of the monarch and gives important powers to Parliament. Since 1689, Parliament has met every year.

The part of the United States Constitution that we call the Bill of Rights was written about a hundred years after the English Bill of Rights. The American Bill of Rights is very different from the English Bill of Rights, however. The American Bill of Rights lists and protects the rights of individual citizens. The English Bill of Rights states some basic rights of Parliament in relation to the monarchy. Parliament at that time consisted mostly of wealthy landowners.

Once these basic rights were established through the Glorious Revolution, however, Parliament continued to claim more rights. The English Bill of Rights was an important step in limiting the power of kings and queens, and in creating a more democratic government in England.

Important Points of the English Bill of Rights

- A ruler is not allowed to set aside laws made by Parliament.

- Parliament must meet frequently.

- The ruler must be a Protestant and cannot marry a Catholic.

- The ruler cannot maintain a standing army in times of peace.

- A ruler cannot collect taxes without the consent of Parliament.

- A ruler cannot interfere with the election of members to Parliament.

- All subjects have the right to **petition** the king.

- A ruler cannot interfere in freedom of speech and debate in Parliament.

- Protestants can bear arms to defend themselves.

- People should not have to pay excessive **bail** or fines, nor should they be given cruel or unusual punishments.

William and Mary accepted the English Bill of Rights, which made it clear that Parliament had gained important powers.

Glossary

A

alliance, n. an agreement between nations in which they work together toward a common goal or fight on the same side in a war (171)

ambassador, n. a person who is an official representative of his or her government in another country (162)

annul, v. to officially state that a marriage never existed under the law (152)

aristocrat, n. a person of the upper or noble class whose status is usually inherited (157)

B

bail, n. money posted to free a prisoner until his or her trial begins (198)

bubonic plague, n. a deadly disease spread by fleas on infected rodents (190)

C

civil war, n. a war between people who live in the same country (174)

compromise, n. when each side in a dispute gives up some of its demands to reach an agreement (187)

convert, v. to change from one belief or religion to another (189)

coronation, n. the ceremony or act of crowning a ruler (150)

"country estate," (phrase), a large home located on a large piece of land in the countryside (174)

current, n. the ongoing movement of water within a larger body of water, such as in a river or ocean (166)

custody, n. imprisonment or protective care (155)

D

dictator, n. a ruler who has total control over the country (183)

disband, v. to end a group or an organization; dissolve (187)

dissolve, v. to end something, such as an organization (183)

"divine right of kings," (phrase), the belief that kings and queens have a God-given right to rule and that rebellion against them is a sin (168)

dub, v. to officially make someone a knight (162)

E

English Channel, n. a body of water between southern England and northern France that connects the North Sea and the Atlantic Ocean (194)

English Parliament, n. the original law-making branch of the English government that is made up of the House of Lords and the House of Commons (155)

F

fugitive, n. a person who runs away or hides to avoid capture (186)

G

galleon, n. a large sailing ship, used as a warship or for trade (160)

gentry, n. people who own land and have high social standing but no titles of nobility (176)

H

heir, n. a person who will legally receive the property of someone who dies; the person who will become king or queen after the current king or queen dies or steps down (196)

M

monarchy, n. a government led by a king or queen (182)

N

nobleman, n. a person of the upper class; an aristocrat (162)

O

official, n. a person who carries out a government duty (173)

P

pageant, n. a show or play usually based on a legend or history (158)

persecute, v. to treat people cruelly and unfairly (153)

petition, v. to ask a person, group, or organization for something, usually in writing (198)

"public policy", (phrase) laws or rules, both written and unwritten, that govern society (182)

R

rank, n. a position in a group or organization (178)

republic, n. a government in which people elect representatives to rule for them (182)

resin, n. a sticky substance that comes from trees and can be lit (164)

Restoration, n. the historical period during which the monarchy was reestablished (187)

ritual, n. an act or series of actions done in the same way in a certain situation, such as a religious ceremony (153)

T

treason, n. the crime of being disloyal to one's own country (180)

Core Knowledge®

CKHG™
Core Knowledge History and Geography™

Series Editor-In-Chief
E.D. Hirsch, Jr.

Editorial Directors
Linda Bevilacqua and Rosie McCormick

The Renaissance

Subject Matter Expert

Ann E. Moyer, PhD, Department of History, University of Pennsylvania

Illustration and Photo Credits

Cover Images: The Globe Theatre, English School, (20th century) / Private Collection / © Look and Learn / Bridgeman Images; Flying Machine, SuperStock/SuperStock

Adoration of the Magi (tempera on panel) (for detail see 315894), Botticelli, Sandro (Alessandro di Mariano di Vanni Filipepi) (1444/5–1510) / Galleria degli Uffizi, Florence, Italy / Bridgeman Images: 18

akg-images/akg-images/SuperStock: 73

Andre Lebrun/age fotostock/SuperStock: 65

Art Archive, The/SuperStock: 3

Atlas, copy of a Greek Hellenistic original (marble) (detail), Roman / Museo Archeologico Nazionale, Naples, Italy / Bridgeman Images: 7

Barnes Foundation/SuperStock: 15

Cosimo de' Medici (Il Vecchio) (1389–1463) 1518 (oil on panel), Pontormo, Jacopo (1494–1557) / Galleria degli Uffizi, Florence, Italy / Bridgeman Images: 26

Don Quixote, English School, (20th century) / Private Collection / © Look and Learn / Bridgeman Images: 86

Exterior view of S. Maria del Fiore, 1294–1436 (photo) / Duomo, Florence, Italy / Bridgeman Images: 28

Fine Art Images/Fine Art Images/SuperStock: 54, 85

Iberfoto/Iberfoto/SuperStock: 77

imageBROKER/imageBROKER/SuperStock: 66

Interior of a 16th century printing works, copy of a miniature from 'Chants royaux sur la Conception couronnee du Puy de Rouen' (colour litho), French School, (16th century) (after) / Bibliotheque Nationale, Paris, France / Bridgeman Images: 47

Lorenzo de' Medici (1449–92) surrounded by artists, admiring Michelangelo's 'Faun' (fresco), Mannozzi, Giovanni (da San Giovanni) (1592–1636) / Museo degli Argenti, Palazzo Pitti, Florence, Italy / Bridgeman Images: 30

Martin Hargreaves: 12–13, 16

Melancholia, 1514 (engraving), Dürer or Duerer, Albrecht (1471–1528) / Private Collection / Bridgeman Images: 80

Merchants meeting to establish fish prices in Venice towards end of century, miniature from Venetian manuscript / De Agostini Picture Library / A. Dagli Orti / Bridgeman Images: 43

Peter Willi/Peter Willi/SuperStock: 71

Pieta by Michelangelo (1475–1564), St Peter's Basilica in Vatican City / De Agostini Picture Library / M. Carrieri / Bridgeman Images: 61

Pope Leo I (c.390–461) Repulsing Attila (c.406–453) 1511–14 (fresco), Raphael (Raffaello Sanzio of Urbino) (1483–1520) /

Vatican Museums and Galleries, Vatican City / Alinari / Bridgeman Images: 35

Portrait of Isabella d'Este (1474–1539), Titian (Tiziano Vecellio) (c.1488–1576) / Kunsthistorisches Museum, Vienna, Austria / Ali Meyer / Bridgeman Images: 48

Portraits of Leo X (1475–1521) Cardinal Luigi de' Rossi and Giulio de Medici (1478–1534) 1518 (oil on panel), Raphael (Raffaello Sanzio of Urbino) (1483–1520) / Galleria degli Uffizi, Florence, Italy / Bridgeman Images: 39

Reconstruction of St. Peter's Basilica and the Piazza from the Plans by Donato Bramante (1444–1514) (w/c on paper), French School, (20th century) / Archives Larousse, Paris, France / Bridgeman Images: 36

Recruitment of Venetian troops on the Molo, c.1562, Angolo del Moro, Gian Battista (1514–75) / Palazzo Ducale, Venice, Italy / Bridgeman Images: 44

Richard Cummins/SuperStock: 5

School of Athens, from the Stanza della Segnatura, 1510–11 (fresco), Raphael (Raffaello Sanzio of Urbino) (1483–1520) / Vatican Museums and Galleries, Vatican City / Bridgeman Images: i, iii, 21

Self Portrait at the Age of Twenty-Eight, 1500 (oil on panel), Dürer or Duerer, Albrecht (1471–1528) / Alte Pinakothek, Munich, Germany / Bridgeman Images: 81

Sistine Chapel Ceiling, 1508–12 (fresco) (post restoration), Buonarroti, Michelangelo (1475–1564) / Vatican Museums and Galleries, Vatican City / Bridgeman Images: 63

Sistine Chapel Ceiling: Libyan Sibyl, c.1508–10 (fresco), Buonarroti, Michelangelo (1475–1564) / Vatican Museums and Galleries, Vatican City / Alinari / Bridgeman Images: 59

Steve Vidler/SuperStock: 9

SuperStock/SuperStock: 50–51, 56, 64

The Banquet of the Monarchs, c.1579 (oil on canvas), Sanchez Coello, Alonso (c.1531–88) / Muzeum Narodowe, Poznan, Poland / Bridgeman Images: 68–69

The 'Carta della Catena' showing a panorama of Florence, 1490 (detail of 161573), Italian School, (15th century) / Museo de Firenze Com'era, Florence, Italy / Bridgeman Images: 22–23

The Globe Theatre, English School, (20th century) / Private Collection / © Look and Learn / Bridgeman Images: 83

The Miracle of the Relic of the True Cross on the Rialto Bridge, 1494 (oil on canvas) (see also 119437), Carpaccio, Vittore (c.1460/5–1523/6) / Galleria dell' Accademia, Venice, Italy / Bridgeman Images: 40–41

The Wool Factory, 1572 (slate), Cavalori, Mirabello (1510/20–72) / Palazzo Vecchio (Palazzo della Signoria) Florence, Italy / Bridgeman Images: 25

Travel Pictures Ltd/Travel Pictures Ltd/Superstock: 82

View of St. Peter's, Rome, 1665 (oil on canvas), Italian School, (17th century) / Galleria Sabauda, Turin, Italy / Bridgeman Images: 32–33

Westend61/Westend61/Superstock: 1, 52

The Reformation

Subject Matter Expert

Ann E. Moyer, PhD, Department of History, University of Pennsylvania

Illustration and Photo Credits

England in the Golden Age

Subject Matter Expert

John Joseph Butt, PhD, Department of History, James Madison University

Illustration and Photo Credits

Cover Image: Queen Elizabeth I, Iberfoto/SuperStock

A Cavalier with a Grey Horse (oil on panel), Calraet, Abraham van (1642–1722)/Apsley House, The Wellington Museum, London, UK/ Bridgeman Images: 174

A Spanish Treasure Ship Plundered by Francis Drake (c.1540–96) in the Pacific (engraving) (later colouration), Dutch School, (16th century) / Private Collection / Bridgeman Images: 161

Arrival of Queen Elizabeth I at Nonsuch Palace, 1598 (hand coloured copper engraving) (detail), Hoefnagel, Joris (1542–1600) / Private Collection / Bridgeman Images: 157

Charles I of England (1600–49) and Queen Henrietta Maria (1609–69) (oil on canvas), Dyck, Anthony van (1599–1641) / Palazzo Pitti, Florence, Italy / Bridgeman Images: 172

Charles II dancing at a ball at court, 1660 (oil on canvas), Janssens, Hieronymus (1624–93) / Royal Collection Trust © Her Majesty Queen Elizabeth II, 2016 / Bridgeman Images: 188

Cromwell and his Ironsides, illustration from 'A History of England' by C.R.L. Fletcher and Rudyard Kipling, 1911 (colour litho), Ford, Henry Justice (1860–1941) / Private Collection / The Stapleton Collection / Bridgeman Images: 179

Mary II (oil on canvas), Wissing, Willem (1656–87) (after) / Scottish National Portrait Gallery, Edinburgh, Scotland / Bridgeman Images: 193

Pantheon/Superstock: 153

Portrait of James VI, 1595 (oil on canvas), Vanson, Adrian (fl.1580–1601) (attr. to) / Private Collection / Photo © Philip Mould Ltd, London / Bridgeman Images: 169

Portrait of Mary I or Mary Tudor (1516–58), daughter of Henry VIII, at the Age of 28, 1544 (panel), Master John (fl.1544) / National Portrait Gallery, London, UK / Bridgeman Images: 153

Portrait of Oliver Cromwell (1599–1658) 1649 (oil on canvas), Walker, Robert (1607–60) / Leeds Museums and Galleries (Leeds Art Gallery) U.K. / Bridgeman Images: 177

Presentation of the Bill of Rights to William III (1650–1702) of Orange and Mary II (1662–94) (engraving), English School / British Museum, London, UK / Bridgeman Images: 199

Prince Charles Edward Stewart, 1732 (oil on canvas), David, Antonio (1698–1750) / Scottish National Portrait Gallery, Edinburgh, Scotland / Bridgeman Images: 185

Puritan, Roundhead (oil on canvas), Pettie, John (1839–93) / Sheffield Galleries and Museums Trust, UK / Photo © Museums Sheffield / Bridgeman Images: 174

Queen Elizabeth I, c.1600 (oil on panel), English School, (16th century) / National Portrait Gallery, London, UK / Bridgeman Images: 151

Shari Darley Griffiths: 171

Stock Montage/Superstock: 147, 163

The Armada being destroyed by English fire ships, McConnell, James Edwin (1903–95) / Private Collection / © Look and Learn / Bridgeman Images: 165

The Great Fire of London, 1666 (print) (see also 53641), Verschuier, Lieve (1630–86) (after) / Private Collection / Bridgeman Images: 190

The Restoration of Charles II (1630–85) at Whitehall on 29 May 1660, c.1660 (oil on canvas), Fuller, Isaac (1606–72) / Private Collection / Bridgeman Images: 187

Tower of London Seen from the River Thames, from 'A Book of the Prospects of the Remarkable Places in and about the City of London', c.1700 (engraving), English School, (18th century) / O'Shea Gallery, London, UK / Bridgeman Images: 154

Travel Pix Collection/Jon Arnold Images/Superstock: 149

Trial of Charles I, English School, (19th century) / Private Collection / © Look and Learn / Bridgeman Images: 181

William III of Great Britain and Ireland (oil on canvas), Kneller, Godfrey (1646–1723) (attr. to) / Scottish National Portrait Gallery, Edinburgh, Scotland / Bridgeman Images: 192

William III, Prince of Orange, Arriving at Brixham, c.1688–99 (oil on canvas), Dutch School, (17th century) / Royal Collection Trust © Her Majesty Queen Elizabeth II, 2016 / Bridgeman Images: 195